The

Heart Of

Connection

DISCLAIMER

This book is presented to you for information purposes and is not a substitution for any professional advice before taking any action on their part. There are some relationship issues that requires more expert intervention then simply reading a book or taking a relationship skills class. Depending on the nature of the issue, it may be more appropriate to seek help from a licensed professional, such a counselor or therapist.

ISBN: 978-1-7366807-1-1 (Print)

ISBN: 978-1-7366807-0-4 (Ebook)

Library of Congress Control Number: 2021903253

TABLE OF CONTENTS

"when you start communicating to change people, you leave a lasting legacy. you profit from your impact, not in spite of it." **123**

"I Speak To Everyone In The Same Way, Whether He Is The Garbage Man Or The President Of The University" --------------- **123**

INTRODUCTION

Man is a social animal, and we need people around us to complete our lives. It's not an emotional statement, but a practical one. Let me explain it like this; you are walking around the block just window shopping and having a relaxing time and you see these most beautiful pair of shoes on the display. You check the price tag and stagger back because it would be a huge splurge if you bought them. What's the first thing that crosses your mind? For me, the first thing I would do is take a picture and send it to my sister who knows my fetish for a good shoe. Do you get the significance of this simple act? It means that you just shared a thought with someone who you know, understands you. It will happen with the smallest things, your desire to share your discoveries, your emotions, your feelings, your thoughts, your successes, your losses are the basic human instinct that we all possess, and which makes us who we are. I personally know many neighbors, colleagues, friends, who are stuck in the constant struggle for survival in their day to day lives but only dream of altering or reorganizing their priorities and recognizing the bonds they have with others. In this simple guide, we will talk about people and their experiences and how to improve your relationships step by step, only making a few changes in the way you interact. But I will tell you this, it will not be easy. But worry not! This book here will help you start with the most basic and simple variations and observations that will lead you in the right direction for your journey to better your relations with people. The best approach is the one that works best for you as there is no one-size-fits-all approach that works for everyone, so you may need to engage in a bit of trial and error to find what is most helpful for your situation.

First of all, we need to talk about what has made you lose closeness in the first place.

I mean you may know some kids around you, and I can essentially declare that kids are the most straightforward and honest beings, until they grow up and are corrupted by the world.

So, what happened? The answer is simple, yet it will hit you right in between your eyes and hopefully open them up, **you stopped making the effort**. Somewhere along with your busy life and your drive for success or maybe due to just plain laziness, you drifted away from the real things in life and started focusing on your accomplishments instead. Unfortunately, our culture respects individual achievement over personal relationships. We're good at finding career success but less than average at connecting with other people. As a result, our relationships suffer more often than we should like. So, read on if you want some major questions answered, need some light shed on issues that have become out of control, or need some insight just for your information so you may use it later in life.

Personal Growth

The first step to help improve your relationships is to recognize yourself. You need to figure your strengths and weaknesses in or order to work with them for the betterment of yourself and those around you. The key is your own mind and the choices you make because everyone around you will get affected by them sooner or later. So, we need to understand ourselves and then work on ourselves for the enhancement and amelioration of the connection we have with others. You should know that,

"Communication is to relationships what breath is to life."

Virginia Satir

CHAPTER 1

Your Values in Life

I am going to intentionally avoid the topic of good or bad values. What should the best values be and how to put in place a value system that will help you succeed. I will do that because values are a personal thing, and no one has the right to dictate what they should be. This is mainly because I don't want to push my idea of good values on my readers. The thing I will focus on is *why* there needs to be value in life. What's the purpose and importance of having values and living by them? Honestly, there are tons of self-help books out there that guide on a great value system, but they don't actually tell you what they are, how to instill them, and what benefits they will have. It's all rather vague and no one can actually answer the questions for you. I believe that the main purpose of having values is that they have been personally selected and accepted by you due to your own circumstances and likes and dislikes.

The main motive of having values is to realize the life you have and keep a set of rules to decide how you will be spending your time and energy. I don't think that the reason for having values is to only stay happy because happiness is a relative term, you can be happy snorting on drugs and that will eventually destroy your life. So, being happy and staying happy shouldn't be the point. Now you'll ask me what the best way to recognize values and how to set a certain value in place for a specific cause. I will do my best to explain and enlighten you all.

There was a childhood friend of mine and she was a daredevil. She would accept challenges and lived every second with excitement and exhilaration. Unfortunately, her parents were more cautious and would pressure her into making 'safe' choices for herself like a stable career and a 9 to 5 job, they were not wrong in wishing safety for their child, it just wasn't who she was. She tried to adapt to that lifestyle and felt stifled by her conditions. One day we all heard that she quit her job and became a travel blogger. She was now traveling the world and experiencing different cultures, braving hard situations on the way. It took her some time to realize that what she valued most in life were adventure and excitement. She was not the one to be tied down by family, kids, or a desk job. Now, I am not saying that these things are confining or bad, I am merely suggesting that she knew her personal values and went for them. Someone may value family more than anything and wouldn't dream of leaving them behind to travel everywhere. It all comes down to personal preferences and that's what we will talk about here. Everybody is different, and what makes one person happy may leave another person feeling anxious or separated. Defining your personal values and then living by them can help you to feel more satisfied and to make choices that make *you* feel content, even if they don't make sense to other people. You'll see how to go about doing that in the discussion below.

Every day, whether you get it or not, you are deciding how to spend your time, your attention, your energy towards something. Your actions are a mirror for your values and no matter what you say or think, it's what you decide to do, makes that thing more valuable than everything else. For example, I can tell you that I value being healthy and my physical and mental health is the most important thing to me but if I choose to eat a couple of donuts daily and do not find time to work out, then my values are pretty much defined, aren't they?

Now, how to recognize those values, right? Let me start by saying that it is not a piece of cake. No, I don't mean literally, I mean metaphorically. You need to gauge your mood and reactions when an action takes place and notice whether you felt good about the happening or felt dismayed and disappointed in yourself. Let me explain, as I mentioned that I may consider myself a health freak, but I don't work out much and eat unhealthy stuff. How does it make me feel? Well in my case, stuffing my mouth with sweet indulgences is extremely satisfying and I am pretty satisfied by my choice but, someone else in my place may also be doing the same thing, with a huge amount of guilt and disappointment in themselves. This means that they only lack motivation and would be much happier actually taking care of their physic and health. But you cannot be aloof of others around you and if choose to let yourself go, which will be because you value laziness, your parents, your partner, or even some of your friends will be affected by your decision because you are not alone. You have to live in a world where you need to interact with people. Unless you move to Antarctica or somewhere equally remote and throw away your phone.

Basically, your personal values are characteristics and behaviors that are important to you. Let me break it down for you further, there are many things we can value, and the options are endless!

We can care about achievement, adventure, courage, creativity, friendship, family, health, honesty, independence, intelligence, love, kindness, empathy, success, wealth, sincerity, security, perfection, peace, and the list goes on. The idea is not to pick a few from my list and be done with it, I am sure you may value some other things that you did not find here. The purpose is for you to explore your heart and soul and look back on your proudest, happiest, most satisfying moments in life and note them down.

Now, there is a very important thing to keep in mind when defining your values. Our values are an extension of ourselves and you may not like what you see there sometimes. Let me explain it more thoroughly, when something good happens either in a general way or to someone you value in life, you feel satisfaction and pride. But if there's someone you don't like or something that you want to get rid of, you wouldn't feel nice when anything great happens to them. It may stem from jealousy, hatred, distrust, wariness, etc. but the feelings aren't positive, and you will feel ashamed by them secretly. In that case, evaluate your reactions deeply and consistently. Is it a one-off thing? If it is, then perhaps the person or situation deserved the negativity you're dishing out. But if it's a habit you've developed then it may originate from self-loathing or self-hatred and believe me when I tell you that this is a ditch that you won't be able to come out of if you've dug yourself in too deep. Exactly as we place importance on anything in our lives, we can also consider ourselves the same way. Thus, self-destruction feels good in some dark way. The person who despises himself feels that he is justly inferior, that he deserves some awful thing to compensate for his own misery. Whether it's through drugs or alcohol or self-harm or even harming others, there's a nasty part of him that seeks out this damage to justify all of the pain and misery he has felt.

On the other hand, Self-love is crucial but not to the extent that you only love yourself and become a self-obsessed, pompous person. You need to be aware of other people's pain and problems and find empathy in situations that involve others.

If you feel that you do not value the right things in life and are feeling an unsurmountable pressure to reevaluate your preferences and a sense of 'self' as you may like to call it, then just take a break from your schedule and simply, pause. Offload some of the daily pressures of your life and judge them from afar, take a moment to consider your priorities and ask yourself if you actually want the life you have or would you like to make some changes. Only then will you be able to restart your journey of considering your values. If we achieve something that we value, we will get a sense of achievement which will, in turn, increase our self-worth in our own eyes. If we lose someone or something we value, we fall into an emotional crisis where we start questioning ourselves and the purpose of life.

Values are the main component of our psychological design and our identity. We are defined by what we choose to find important in our lives and by our prioritizations. If wealth is the most important thing in our lives, then that will characterize who we are.

Now, that you've recognized and established your values, you realize that some of them are not so beneficial. What will you do?

You cannot argue with someone to change their values. Period. There are no two ways about it. They need to learn to gauge the worth of their values by themselves, as I said at the start, it's a personal choice. They need to experience for themselves that choosing money as a value may not be so beneficial in the long run for them. Let's say that there was a guy who thought money was everything and he chased his whole life after it. When he reached 40, he had a pretty good amount saved up but, he didn't feel any happiness or sense of satisfaction. Now he realizes that running after money was not something that he should have done his whole life and should have built some other values for himself because you eventually turn your values into goals. That's a given. He wishes at that moment that he had other, *better* values put in place.

He should have given his kids more time or had gone on vacations more. The process of maturity is key to analyze your mistakes and place value in more rewarding things. He may need to replace his drive for money to drive for freedom. Financial freedom is something that we should all value, by the way. Just saying.

When you do gather the courage to live out your new values it feels good. Once you experience those benefits, not only does it become easier to continue living the new value, but you feel like a fool because you didn't do this sooner. It's like going out on a chilly morning for a jog, you are terrified of the cold and have absolutely no desire to feel the anguish in your legs but afterward, you feel the exhilaration and love every minute of it. You're left with a wonderful sense of relief, and a newer, deeper understanding of who you really are.

Another great personal value is guilt. You need to have a sense of guilt at making mistakes in your life and then learning from them. As long as you have guilt, you can keep yourself in check. You can take account of all the rights and wrongs and noticing your errors can modify them until you are guilt-free. This helps in developing a connection with people and you start valuing the human interactions that you will experience throughout your life. I have yet to meet a single person who doesn't value another person in life, no matter who that person is. It can be a friend, a relative, your boss, or someone that you really look up to. It can only be one figure, but everyone needs someone to survive. Our world is built in such ways. That's why we need to take care of the people we value and try to make our relationship stronger with them.

In the end, you need to know that you cannot win in every situation or become the best at everything. Whenever you find yourself straying from your values, analyze the situation afterward and ask yourself what you could have done differently.

We need to choose our battles wisely and probably aim for the affection for a few people in our lives, instead of winning over everyone.

The simplest advice I can give you is to follow your gut. Whatever feels right, that would be the value you most care about, so you'll be happiest following your instincts.

CHAPTER 2

Slay the Ego.

N ow that we have established a set of values that you most likely feel are very important to you. How will you use them to improve the relationships you have in life? After all, that's the purpose of the whole book, right? So, after your values are recognized, the next step is to work on the biggest problem, the elephant in the room and that no one dares to address. We need to slay the dragon. Yes! You read it right. Your ego. It needs to go.

But firstly, let me explain what's ego. To be egotistical means that you would be deemed somewhat negatively but to have elevated degrees of self-esteem is positive. People with massive egos are continually insecure and are trying to cover up those insecurities by pretending to be serious or better than everyone else. People with big egos have a shortage of confidence and self-love. Now don't get me wrong here, we all have an ego. But, we must learn to control it and prevent it from taking over our personality. If you let your ego go unrestrained, it can cause enormous upheaval in your life particularly with your partner, someone you share your home with or your spouse. According to statistics, almost 90% of our relationships are negatively affected by our inflated egos.

Let me tell you a story of a woman I knew when I was young. She was a neighbour of mine but in those days, we had neighbours who were practically family. She used to visit my mom every day and I will not call them friends because they were a little closer than that. They would exchange recipes and cook and send each other's favourite foods. Babysit the other's kids and all that good stuff. We were so close that we were all on a first-name basis with each other. I was fond of Margret and I really believed that she was an aunt of mine until I was much older and found out the truth of our relationship. The thing I most remember about her is that she would relentlessly complain about her husband. Nonstop. It was like a hobby of hers and she did it funnily so we all would laugh but, the point was that she was never happy with anything the poor man did. Now, we don't know this for sure, but I believe that she would badger him with criticisms at home too. I say this because one day, he packed his bags and just left. Being the naive kid that I was, I thought that she would be actually happy now that he was gone but I was shocked to find out that she was devastated. She cried and wailed and mourned for him like he was dead. I wasn't very close with Uncle Steve but even I felt his loss because of how much Margret missed him. My mom urged her to call him, but she would refuse. She told my mother that she will never call him herself and that that would be the last thing she would ever have done. As I said, kids are the most honest beings, and we are pretty straight forward so we don't see the tricks the mind plays on adults. I couldn't understand her reason for not calling her husband back when clearly, she loved him to bits. She pined away for him until we moved houses years later and Margret was still waiting for him to come back. We tried to keep in touch, but our busy schedules just let us drift apart and we lost contact completely.

I still think about her sometimes, she was the classic case of an Egoistic person and she destroyed her married life because of it. She lost the most important person in her life and couldn't tell him that she loved him because of her ego. It ruined her but she still held on to it.

So, this is what we need to avoid in our lives. This is the most damaging trait to have and it will hurt you in the long run. Negative emotions like jealousy, hatred, and insecurity are all results of an out-of-control ego.

I have seen ego ruin lives and I am a witness to its destruction. My sister's best friend was a sweet and creative girl who knew how to have fun. At one of her parties, she met a guy who she fell in love with. It was like instant combustion and I cannot say that it wasn't from both sides. We all could see that the guy was also head over heels for her. They got married within six months and started a life together. Then the problems started. She wanted to grow up and live a grounded life with him, but he wouldn't hear any of it and continued his life like before, partying and wasting away their money, finally cheating on her again and again. She forgave everything. For a long time, we witnessed the charade from the side-tracks until my sister decided to have a little talk with her friend but, little did she know that she was in for a reality check. The friend wouldn't listen to anything, she refused to even talk about it. She told my sister in no uncertain terms that if any of her friends spoke poorly about her husband, she would immediately cut off all ties with them. The threat worked and we let her be, but we couldn't see her disappearing right in front of our eyes and we started walking away from the tragedy that was her life. Cruel, I know but not more than what she was subjecting herself to. So, what was stopping her from accepting the truth and facing up to the reality of her situation? Love? No. It was her ego. She couldn't possibly love someone who would hurt her so blatantly and break her heart so many times. She was afraid of letting go because her ego was battered. I always tell my sister that it wasn't the guy who broke her it was her ego.

Oftentimes a person will remain in a bad relationship because her ego won't allow her to accept that her judgment of her partner's character was wrong. The ego is bruised, and she can't accept that she was less attractive or less desirable than her husband's girlfriend. It couldn't be true that she invested years into a relationship that isn't working out.

Our ego won't allow us to accept the situation. So, we hang on to the lie to prove that we are worthy enough.

For the egotist, being right all the time is closely associated with feeling valuable. Hence, people who can't let go of their egos would do and say anything they can to be deemed correct. Unfortunately, this happens at the cost of everything else. The need to always be right and the fear of being wrong in the eyes of others can ruin relationships with co-workers, bosses, siblings, friends, relatives, and spouses.

If you let go of your ego and those fears, you can live your life without limits and accomplish a lot more. To battle with the fear of rejection, you need to love yourself and know that you deserve positivity in your life. You must accept that life is running side by side with failures. Stop defending yourself because you cannot be right every time. And that's okay. We are humans and are bound to make mistakes. But our strength lies in what we did after making that mistake. Acknowledging if you are at fault and then trying to make up for it is the best way to deal with difficult situations and perfect for self-realization. Sometimes it's an acceptance that you need not the defense. Gaining control of your ego is the best thing that you can do for yourself.

Forgiveness is the fundamental part of interacting with people. You need to begin with being more tolerant and stop taking offenses. Not everyone knows how to have an ideal conversation every time and someone might make a blooper someday. Sometimes they would say things that they didn't mean. Sometimes both the parties would be disagreeing on certain things but both of them would be right in their own way. You won't be able to understand why people do what they did unless you put yourself in their shoes. If you feel that some problem can be found, then talk about it. Talk about problems and get done with them, right then and there. You shouldn't expect someone to come and solve them for you when you haven't even confessed that you're facing a problem. Don't let your ego come in the way of common sense.

The best advice I have for you to tackle your ego is, Text first, call first, talk first, say sorry first, it doesn't make you a loser. If you love the person, then take the first step. No matter who is right or wrong, the person in your life should be more important than thinking who is going to apologize first and deciding between who's right or wrong. Life is more than that so please let go of the petty issues and relax and enjoy yourselves.

CHAPTER 3

Be Optimistic and Encouraging

T his is a trait that is fulfilling and rewarding and would let you achieve almost anything in life. Trust me. I will teach you a lesson that you'll remember for a long time.

One day, I was sitting in a café, enjoying my morning latte when came bustling in a mother and daughter duo. The girl would have been about 11 or 12 years old. The mother had a very angry expression on her face and the poor kid's whole demeanour was wired with tension. She had lost in a competition at school and her mom was disappointed in her. Both of them were sitting to my left and I couldn't help but overhear their conversation or rather one-sided discussion. The mom was extremely upset and it's understandable to be dispirited when one has put in a lot of effort and has much higher expectations. But she kept humiliating the child relentlessly and I couldn't do anything about it because after all, it was between a mother and a daughter, who was I to interfere? Nonetheless, I felt very bad for the girl and tried to pretend that I couldn't hear anything so that the child wouldn't get embarrassed further. "How could you be so stupid Alicia?" The mother's nasal voice reached my ears and my blood started boiling. I felt very upset but didn't have the authority to do anything. She kept on going and addressed her child with mean titles. They finished their meal and left but I was left with a huge amount of empathy for the child. The way the mother had treated her daughter was not right.

A situation will arise where you would find yourself facing huge losses and you will either feel disappointed in yourself or someone else but the key is to stay positive, keep an optimistic approach and keep on encouraging. If the mother had encouraged her instead of absolutely crushing her confidence, then the girl might have entered another competition with refreshed goals. But you never know, she may have gotten inspired to remove her mother's dismay, and the need to please her may have increased. All I'm saying is that a little bit of encouragement goes a long way.

Let's suppose that you have recently acquired a passion for baking and you think you do a decent job. Your brother's coming to visit you and you decide to bake brownies for him, knowing that he loves those. But when your brother takes a bite, he makes a horrible face and spits out the rest. "These are awful! Please stop baking. You're wasting expensive ingredients, sis." You will feel devastated. Not only has your brother completely ravaged your feelings, but he has also razed your confidence to the ground. Now, you may have completely butchered the brownies or they may have come out pretty decent. That's not the point, the essence of my story is that you will probably not try to bake anything for anyone ever again.

We often face negative situations and encounter negative people and are regularly introduced to bad news through media and social media. How is it possible to stay positive in such a sad environment? What should you do? Let me tell you. The key is to keep a positive frame of mind. I know it's not easy but I will share a secret with you. Positivity is contagious. It is a fact. You can test it out if you don't believe me. By being around positive people, gradually, you will notice that you are becoming positive too. I had seen this documentary a few years ago which endorsed the idea of using positive thoughts to attract more positivity in your life. At the time I didn't really think the idea would work but now I have seen it happen and have been a witness to this theory. It's not hard to practice it as well but yes, once faced with negative situations that are practically unavoidable in life sometimes, how to stay on the positive side of things instead of getting swept away by the negative vibes.

The answer is that you can learn to stay positive in negative situations. However, this requires caution, awareness of your thoughts, and some personal rethinking. It may need a lot of practice over time but it is actually a fun activity to try. Try to find solutions instead of focusing on the problems. The most positive people I know would distance themselves from feelings of failure and concentrate on looking for a way to make the situation better. If we are persistent, the answers come to us sooner or later.

I had a colleague and we were on friendly terms. I cannot call him a friend because we weren't that close but we used to see each other almost daily in the office where I worked a long time ago and we were cordial. He was a runner and used to run for marathons. We would go to his events to support him sometimes and he was actually pretty lithe and fast. I used to tell my sister that I wish I had a healthy hobby like him so that I could become fit while enjoying myself. We used to laugh at the concept of me running for miles as a hobby. Anyway, Micheal, that's his name, was driving to work one day when he had an accident and got injured severely. When he didn't show up for work the next day too, we all got a call from his partner telling us what had happened. A group of office workers decided to visit him in the hospital after work and I also went along with them. I couldn't believe my eyes! The guy who was so tall and fit looked like a small kid lying on the bed. He had scratches all over his face and hands but the major part of the trauma was an injury to his spine. He was motionless from the waist down. The doctors told him that he probably wouldn't be able to walk again. I don't know how he had felt at that moment, but I was hit by a thunderbolt. I couldn't believe it! What would he do? How will he survive this? These thoughts were running through everyone's mind. I am sure he was crushed and couldn't think clearly. We all went back to our lives and got busy with our routines but at the back of my mind, I would always have this feeling of despondence whenever I saw his empty desk. A month later he joined the office again, in a wheelchair. We all welcomed him back but the air was heavy with sadness. At least he is back to work, poor guy. That was what I had been thinking but boy was I wrong. One day at lunch he told everyone that he had been working with a physiotherapist daily and had been successful in wiggling his toes. It was still a far cry from sprinting but according to the doctors, it was a miraculous recovery. We all congratulated him but the thing that I noticed was, he was extremely optimistic about his situation and was in a good frame of mind. I was very happy for him and before we knew it, he was swimming with a trainer, using his arms and then one final day he sauntered into the office on his own two feet. We were delighted to see him and I had actual tears in my eyes. I left the job soon after but we kept in touch through social media and remarkably, he is running again, not at marathons, but with his partner in a park. The only thing I took away from this story and that I want you all as well, is to focus on is this guy's optimism. He didn't give up and didn't accept the situation that he had been put in by a freak accident. He fought and persevered and in the end, he got what he deserved. I still feel goosebumps thinking about his struggle and his journey to recovery.

Keeping yourself motivated through positive affirmations is very important. Micheal would also mutter them whenever he thought he couldn't go on. He would say, just one more step. I can keep exercising for another minute, and he would keep going. I want to inspire you all by sharing his amazing story so that you understand that nothing is impossible if you have an optimistic approach and a positive mindset. Stay away from negative people and join the company of people or groups that will inspire you to be better. This will help you make friends and stop you from repelling people with your negative comments. It will help you become an anchor for your loved ones and they will gravitate towards you whenever they needed a boost of confidence or a nugget of happiness.

You cannot avoid poor conditions or a negative atmosphere but you can strive to stay positive and keep people around you the same.

It needs a lot of practice, perseverance, and a lot of self-love and inner work but in the end, you get to be the constructive influence on other's lives.

Now, the important thing to keep in mind is that you will meet certain people who are not on the journey of self-growth and their personal values are wrong for the moment. These people will want to dampen your vibe and would try to suffocate your encouraging support. They will point out all the things that can go wrong and being mere humans, you can become nervous sometimes. They will also subject you to a lot of cruelty and will make you feel embarrassed and unworthy. Strive not to take personally, what people think and say about you. There is no reason in the world to allow their thoughts and words to hurt you. It is you, who allow their thoughts and words to affect how you feel. Often, people are not even aware that they hurt you, they are just coming from a place where they haven't been taught to love themselves and spread kindness, it's not their fault and they are just the way they are. Sometimes, you could be mistaken too. They might have meant something different and you misunderstood them. They might have been joking, or what they said was not about you at all. In any case, just keep your head down, smile, and move on.

Other things like meditation and regular exercise will help you clear your thoughts and stay positive and optimistic. While meditation might now be everyone's cup of tea but this practice for only 10 minutes every day will relieve your stress and help you relax and think of better solutions for the issues you may have to face. You can also do any kind of exercise whether it is swimming, walking, playing a sport but if you're not used to daily workout then start slowly and build your stamina gradually. Once you are in a better place in your mind, people around you, either strangers or your loved ones, will be happier too. Let me leave you with a few quotes from smart people who know how to live their lives with their families and friends.

"Optimism is the opium of the people."

Milan Kundera

"Optimism is a happiness magnet. If you stay positive, good things and good people will be drawn to you."

Mary Lou Retton

Take inspiration from this quote by - *Peter Daisym*

"I start each day by telling myself what a positive influence I am on this world."

CHAPTER 4

No Complaints and Criticism

The stark truth of the matter is, no one likes a complainer. Period. This is something that's a hundred percent given and you can't argue about it with anyone. No matter how much love and affection is there between two people, once the complaints start, things will start going downhill from there. It can be anyone you're close to, even when your parents start complaining a little too much, you'll feel the prick of irritation and would want to escape the scene. It happens with everyone so you're not alone. Now, if you become labeled as a complainer, would you like the feeling? I don't think so. Let me tell you a story.

A friend of mine has a cousin and she told me the incident that happened with him that we all should take lessons from. He was a nice guy and was just your ordinary, college-going, and living life to the fullest, kind of person. But, he developed this habit of criticizing people around him, whether friends or family, he would just bash them up and complain about their every act. It was ok with friends who would meet him once a week but the more the interaction grew, the more people started avoiding him. He would complain to his siblings and family that his friends were changing and didn't want to hang out anymore. Of course, the typical bias of the family system requires us to always take the side of our own flesh and blood even if they're in the wrong so, no one would really point out this awful habit of his and would sympathize with him readily. Things started taking a turn for the worst when he came back home from the college as the campus was closed due to the COVID-19 situation. He was at home 24/7 and his bad nature started affecting the relationship he had with his parents, especially his mom. As she worked from home, both of them spent a solid amount of time in each other's company and she got the brunt of his tactlessness. He would criticize her cooking skills and her cleaning habits. He would complain about his friends' changing behaviors, he would whine about his campus being closed and about the Coronavirus, anything that would come to his mind would be moaned about. It became so bad that his mom couldn't even stand with him for five whole minutes. She would try to avoid her own son but because he was so critical, she started taking his criticism to heart and actually started believing the accusations he made about her personally. As she was also homebound and was feeling upset by the uncertainty of the situation around her, she began falling into a state of mild depression. It started with small bouts of sadness but grew into more strong and negative emotions. The guy, clueless about his mother's feelings, kept on with his terrible habit, and one final day it all came crashing down on everyone's head. She took a handful of pills and tried to commit suicide. She was taken to the hospital in time and was saved by this tragedy but, the son got a reality check of such an astronomical level that he was flabbergasted. His father, who knew what had been transpiring but was unable to control his son's acidic words, came forward and told him the truth finally. The poor boy was so ashamed that he couldn't even make eye contact with anyone after that. He apologized to his mother after that and altered his habitual complaining and controlled his instincts entirely. They got a close call but thankfully were saved from irrevocable damage.

Habitual criticism can corrode the very foundation of a relationship and I am not trying to be overly dramatic here. I am merely stating a fact.

But, no one is going to expect you to roll over and accept all the negativity dished out for you without any objections. You need to be able to convey your message or your feedback in words that should not be insulting or degrading. You need to make sure that you don't hurt anyone's feelings in the process of being honest about your opinions. You should be able to tell your partner, friend, or neighbour, whoever is the subject of your problem, what you think, or how you feel without criticizing them as an individual.

The key is to *not make it personal*. If you attack someone personally instead of identifying the flaw in their behavior or act, then it can lead to hard feelings and shattered egos which will give rise to other emotional imbalances and will eventually impact your relationship with the person.

According to a therapist, healthy feedback is about the behavior and not the person. When your observations include cursing or demeaning titles, it kills any value your message has and makes your viewpoints pointless. Your words will fall on deaf ears because of how they are spoken. Just like the guy we discussed previously. He may have been right about some things that were being conducted incorrectly but, as it had become his habit to criticize, he had offended everyone around him with his toxic nature. As a result, no one took his words seriously and we're repulsed by him.

Our critical side tends to rear its ugly head during heated moments of stress, making it a difficult habit to crack. But understanding the effect it has on your relationship with people and the impression that you make on others, may force you to reconsider your habits.

If you have been been on the receiving end of criticism then you would know, that these words cut deep. Repeated criticism may shake your confidence and eventually make you doubt your ability to do things right.

Knowing this, you would never want to intentionally subject your loved ones to this torture. Your relations would trust you. As they believe that you mean them no harm, they can begin to believe that since you care about them, then what you're saying about them must be true.

Relentless criticism will create a gap between you are the other person and the warm, loving feeling will be replaced by misgivings and hostility. Once one wring act takes place, then there's no stopping the tirade of wrongdoings as a result. People usually forget who had started it first but the essential thing that remains is to one-up the other person. Which will destroy every kind of relationship.

Constantly criticizing the other person means that you consider yourself superior and more knowledgeable than them. You think you know better and you are the best at everything which goes to show your own mental inability to accept the truth. This tactic is often used by emotional abusers who feed off of other people's insecurities and anxieties.

But, don't get disheartened just yet, you or the other person may not be necessarily discouraging or emotionally abusing each other. People who complain sometimes, may not mean to insult. They may have a crude way of pointing out an obvious problem. For instance, many of us have called our partners, or family members lazy when they just want to lie down in front of the TV and become couch potatoes. It most certainly doesn't mean that we were being critical freaks and were planning to demean them. It just suggests that we were needing help with some household chores and wanted them to take an interest in some chores. An occasional onslaught of name-calling is acceptable because we all get frustrated sometimes and well we're just humans. But, if it becomes a habit then it can lead to emotional and psychological abuse. So what do you do if, unfortunately, you have developed this offensive habit and want to get rid of it?

Being honest is the answer to your question. Being critical is different from complaining about something fundamental. Criticism is personal but occasional complaints are behavioural. The criticism stems from your needs and is the misguided attempt to request someone fulfil them. The most important part is to express your feelings, start your sentences with *I feel* or *I need*. Make sure the other person understands the significance of your request and how much it means to you.

You are so ungrateful! I work two jobs and you can't even appreciate when I cook and clean for you! This statement right here is the deal-breaker. It may be true to an extent and surely expresses your feelings but it will anger the other person rather than consider your efforts which is what you wanted in the first place.

Honey! I put a lot of effort into this dish. Why don't you try it and give me your honest opinion? Your appreciation means a lot to me.

This will make your loved one reconsider their response and would make him or her appreciate the effort and love you put into the act.

Why don't you help out with the kids?! Dishing out an insult like this will provoke the other person into becoming defensive. Choose your words by being sympathetic towards your loved ones.

I know you work very hard but I wish you would sometimes pick the kids from school to lighten my load a little.

This will enlighten them to take your burdens into account and not focus on their own schedule all the time.

The other thing to keep in mind is that to stop yourself from complaining insistently, you will try to neglect the issues that are bothering you which can lead to a lot of mental stress. You don't want to come across as a criticizer and that fine, but not speaking up about something that's bothering you can also end up souring a relationship permanently. Don't let your feelings fester and express your true emotions and intentions but do it in a way that will help you solve the problem instead of giving birth to another one. People usually go on a rant once they have become deeply disturbed and do not find a way to vent their feelings. This can inflict pain and make you grow distant from your loved one.

My advice is that don't carry the weight of your unsaid feelings unnecessarily and speak up but do so gently and with the utmost respect for your relation. As they say, you catch more flies with honey than you do with vinegar.

CHAPTER 5

Be Genuinely Interested

———————❈———————

Genuine interest is one of the most important aspects of a good relationship. It actually makes a world of difference between two people and their connection with each other. In all of my interactions with people and my discussions with the ones who I think communicate well with others, this concept has proven itself over and over again. I can stress the importance of this one-act enough. It can take you from a detached and reticent relationship to a close and attentive one. It also shows what kind of a person you are and sometimes all it takes is that one observation about your own response to others' needs that will help you make the change. Think about it for a second. You're with a good friend who you think cares about your feelings. You are telling her about how much fun you had last night with your family. You delve into a story about how your mom was having difficulty pouring wine into glasses and how it was flying everywhere. You recall the incident and laugh at the absurdity of the situation. You glance at your friend to see if she also gets the humour and expect to see her laughing with you but as soon as you see her preoccupied expression you get a jolt of surprise. She was never listening to you but lost in her own world or probably getting bored. You might have been talking about running away with monkeys and she wouldn't have known. How would you feel? You will possibly be extremely hurt by her lack of interest in you and your life and it will most probably make you renounce the spark of connection that you had with your friend before. Now, it can be a one-time thing, and maybe she is actually under some kind of mental stress. But, if you know that she is ok and was just not bothered to pay attention to you then that means your friendship will suffer the consequences. Imagining this will help you figure out the mistakes you make while interacting with people and never lose a relationship because of your reservedness.

When you start following a script instead of inquiring about their lives then things become remotely uncomfortable. It's like that poor soul is trying to have a conversation with a robot who is programmed to ask him a set of questions without listening to the answers. It is a pretty weird feeling and something that will not build any real connection with you.

So what should you do? How should you work on yourself? Let me elaborate.

Rapport is a skill that some lucky people pick up naturally and are very good at. But it's something which most of us have to learn and work on to hone our skills. This is a very important and helpful ability to create a connection with almost everyone. It is a key to successful relationships and being popular with strangers too. But what if this doesn't come naturally to you and you can't strike a conversation with just about anyone? Then you need to keep a few simple things in mind. Show interest. By your behavior, expression and response, let the other person know that you care, even if you don't agree with them.

Let me tell you about my uncle. He is one of the most popular people in my family and everyone wants to spend some time with him. I always wondered why Uncle Sam was so famous and liked and got my answer after observing his conversations with others. He would sit with kids and talk about video games and pop culture, he would have pretty good knowledge about those topics and would show a lot of excitement for them. He would sit with the ladies and talk about food and recipes and soap operas and would listen to their stories one after the other. He is an example of someone who has mastered the skill of creating rapport between himself and others and what I have seen is that he is not fake. He is actually quite interested in other people's lives. He is the same with everyone and can spend hours talking to anyone. He is truly a marvellous and caring person who has a wonderful relationship with his family and friends.

According to my observation, there are two kinds of people. One who is actually interested in what you're saying, like Uncle Sam, and the other who treat you as an audience to rant about their own experiences and have no interest in a two-way conversation. You will find that and the latter to be aloof and disinterested in your story but as soon as you pause to take a breath they will jump in and begin telling you about their experience. Then they become animated and enthusiastic and probably maintain relatively stable eye contact with you.

But if you attempt to talk about something else and give your input, they change - and the change is often quite sudden. You get The Treatment: they become quiet, the eye contact is reduced, they become still, and any comments they make are perfunctory or are made distractedly. They lose interest in you because they are not in the limelight anymore. Their lack of encouraging responses will potentially have the effect of what the Behaviourists call 'extinguishing the behavior' i.e. deterring you from continuing to talk about your views. After some time you would just lose the enthusiasm to continue the topic and will eventually shut up and let them continue with their story. Which is exactly what they wanted. There will be a lot of signals for you to notice and realize that you have been treated by such a person.

Impatience: they will make lots of impatient sounds to hurry you along: 'Uh, huh' or 'Yeah. Yeah. Yeah' in a brisk manner so that you can just get on with it and hurry up.

Expression: they will tend to break eye contact a lot and look around or adopt an impassive and uninterested look.

Behavior: they will shift their feet, look at their watch, cross and uncross their arms, scratch their heads, and keep nodding feverishly just to convey that they are not interested in what you're saying.

Jumping in: if you pause to take a breath, they jump in with their own comment and then take the conversation off in a different direction with a raised voice and animated hand gestures to let you know that there is no room for interruption.

Dismissive Bess: they will dismiss your opinion either crudely by saying things like *what nonsense!* Or *I don't think so*. Or would use subtle hints like *mmhm right, but what I think.*

You need to avoid being one of these egotistical people and stay away from becoming an uninterested, indifferent and uncaring human being. How? Let's see. Suppose you are talking to someone, and you find yourself being really bored. How do you turn it around and make the conversation interesting by showing genuine interest?

The answer is – you don't! Take a moment and think about what genuine interest means. It's genuine interest! That's real interest in the person or subject matter that's being discussed. There are a set of things you are really interested in that are tied to your feelings. This is not something you can change in a few minutes, or even over months or years. You just can't have a genuine interest when you're not excited by the topic.

The thing is, you already know how to show genuine interest in the n things you care about. If I'm interested in reading, I ask questions about books I've read, books I want to read, etc. Every single person already does this part really well. It's the people and their emotions that you need to develop the connection with. If you value a person in your life then you would pay attention to what they are saying. Period.

We have all been the ones to change a topic if doesn't appeal to us but start another topic that you might be eager about and listen to what your friend, co-worker, or partner is saying. Value their opinions and agree or disagree with their observations. In short, pay attention and make them feel like you're genuinely interested in their lives.

CHAPTER 6

Listen and Understand

N ow that we have established that genuine interest is the main component to establish a healthy relationship, the skill that follows automatically is your listening skill. Not only do you need to listen attentively to others, but you should also understand where they are coming from and what they actually need from you.

How do you feel when someone you love ignores you and your ramblings about any number of issues that you are looking about? Would you honestly feel a connection with someone who purposely dismisses your sentiments? I don't think so. As the saying goes, don't do unto others what you don't want for yourself. Or something along those lines. Anyway, my point is that you really want to learn to be attentive if you want your people to know that you care. Listening strengthens relationships and demonstrates attentiveness, caring, and respect. However, listening isn't limited to hearing. It's much more than that. To truly listen, you must give your undivided attention and put your own plans and needs aside.

Good listening is an active process. For some, it comes naturally, like creating a natural rapport, but many have to learn and practice the valuable skill of thoughtful and conscious listening. There a few things that need to be kept in mind while exercising your listening skills.

Do not interrupt. Interrupting someone is a frequent mistake people make, especially if they have known each other for some time. It may happen without the motive to undermine the other's idea or knowledge but it can cause disrespect and may feel insulting. Our first impulse often involves jumping right into a conversation before the other person has finished talking. While you might think you are actively involving yourself with the other person's problem, you may be limiting or halting that person's ability to communicate. Keep silent until that person pauses for a response from you.

We are often consumed by our own ideas and thoughts and cannot wait to pitch our own wisdom and reasoning for a situation that we can overlook other people's input. People mostly interrupt to pitch in their own story and compete in the storytelling. Some may feel that sharing a related story is proof you were listening, but instead, it may appear that you are trying to steal the show, not to mention, it shows that you have little interest in what they have to say. Common examples are "You should hear about what happened to me!" or "I went through something related to this but much worse!". This kind of attitude would land you on thinner ice and you will not be able to connect with anyone on a deeper level.

Try and not to make assumptions or create your opinions until you have a complete understanding of the situation while listening to your friend or family member. Assuming involves having preconceived notions about the topic being communicated. Sometimes listening involves clarifying not only what the person says but what he or she means.

Verify your conception of the viewpoint before jumping to conclusions prematurely. Similarly, do not discount or dismiss other's emotions. Try to appreciate the philosophy, even if you don't agree with it. That is what good listeners do. They just listen, but there are a few things that you need to add to the listening process.

Listen from your heart and empathize. Showing empathy is recognizing and appreciating the situation. Words like "I can see how that would feel" show you are listening to the emotion behind the statements and recognize the depth of sensitivities behind them. Also, do not force your agenda; put it aside for the time. Listen for comprehension, not consensus. Your turn to present your ideas will be offered later. But while listening, clear your mind and give your full attention. Give them your full attention. Concentrate on their utterances and do not get distracted by anything that may give the signal of lack of interest. Stop whatever you're doing and make eye contact and take full notice of their feelings and words. It's a good idea to ask as many questions as you can to make the story more understandable. For the purpose of clarity, if you need some questions answered then ask away but keep in mind that you need to be respectful and are only inquiring so that you get the hang of the whole situation. Do not condemn or downplay someone's emotions for the sake of humor or to show off your wit. It is acceptable to ask what the other person needs from you while they are discussing something, especially if you want to know how you can be of help. Does the other person just want to vent, do they want to be understood or do they need ideas? Even if they want to vent off their feelings, the fact that they've chosen you to talk about it is nothing short of an honor. Respect their feelings and try to measure up to their expectations by providing them with your undivided attention. Lastly, patience is key. You need to remain patient, even if it's something you rarely practice, and let them speak their heart out. Remain silent until an opinion is requested and then provide useful insight. Allow the other person to finish their thoughts and their statements before jumping in with any response. You may encounter outbursts of emotions. Hot topics often involve raised voices and emotional outbursts. If you want to empathize, you've got to maintain a neutral persona and let them get their feelings off their chests before the intervention.

Good communication is crucial to a loving and healthy relationship. Being able to openly communicate and also believe that you have been heard is significant to the success of a resilient friendship, marriage, or any other relationship. Effective listening is essential to good communication but nowadays, speaking has taken the lead and listening had become one of the backbenchers. I believe that listening has much more potential to benefit your relationships than anything else. People who have the patience to listen to others most definitely enjoy contentment and success in any relationship. If you just give your time and provide your interest, you can achieve much more. By just being there you get a better understanding of the needs of your loved ones. The more we understand about one another, the less we fear and the more we are open to love. Let me tell you the story of my cousin's mother-in-law. She was a very quiet lady as she belonged to Asian culture. She was very sweet and kind and would be ready to feed you food whenever you went to visit them. I had the opportunity to meet her a few times because I had taken up some project with my cousin and would drop his wife at her parents' house. My cousin then told me that Manila, which is his mother-in-law, and his father-in-law were having difficulties in their marriage. I was rightfully shocked because I couldn't imagine anyone being more submissive than Manila. I naturally assumed that the fault is with her husband and started defending her in front of my cousin but I was shocked when I found out that it wasn't him. It was her. She was so preoccupied with her household chores and cooking that she barely spent time with her husband anymore. Although, they had lived a good part of their lives together but had not been able to develop a connection. In the beginning, the husband was busy with work but now that he had retired and was at home more, he needed someone to share his experiences and all the small daily undertakings. She just didn't listen to anything he had to say. She had built a shell around herself and had entrapped herself in it. Her poor listening and concentrating skills gave birth to problems at home and I got really upset with their situation. I prayed for the betterment and improvement of their relationship. After a few weeks, I thankfully got to know that they have been going to therapy and had been working on building their relationship. Their therapist had also worked to improve their communication techniques by focusing on her listening skills. They have been seeing gradual progress but the fact that Manila had trouble listening to her husband's complaints or inner feelings, who she has spent her whole life with and probably loves and respects a lot, is of utmost concern. It shows that this issue can arise in almost anyone's life and needs to be replaced sad immediately. Otherwise, it can shake up the foundations of the most stable of relationships.

So you see, relationships are a two-way road. You need to be able to listen respectfully to one another and communicate your feelings for a relationship to thrive. To do this, it's important to be an active listener and really pay attention to your partner, friend, or family member.

Relationship listening skills involve give and take. To truly improve relationships, you may need to ask for help or provide assistance wherever it's required. Let me state a few key points.

Listen to not only what is being said but also to what may not be said. This may include fears, doubts, concerns, and even dreams.

Listen respectfully, no matter how angry you might be!

Start off your responses by reiterating a general misgiving of the other person to show that you have been listening.

It's been said that one of the most common reasons why people see therapists is to have their stories heard. To have your story heard, you need to have a listener. Listening and empathy skills are the basis of good communicators, leaders, and therapists. Listening skills can be learned, but the reality is, some people just tend to be better listeners than others. It's ok if you find it hard. For some, developing good relationship listening skills is difficult to do. Many relationships fail simply due to a lack of communication. Sometimes, simply talking to a therapist, just like Manila, or attending a seminar is all you need to do to jumpstart your relationship. In this day and age, we are truly lucky to have the help we may need in getting back on track as a person or as a partner in a relationship.

If you wish to be listened to as well then just practice what you preach. Listening is the most effective way to bring about growth and change. Those who are heard tend to be more open, more democratic in their approach, and are often less defensive. Good listeners abstain from making judgments and provide a safe environment for speakers.

By listening carefully when someone speaks, we're telling them that we care about what they're saying. It's also important to remember that listening is contagious. When we listen to others, then chances are they will be more inclined to listen to us. The good news is that we can learn to be better listeners; however, listening takes practice. The more we do it, the better we get at it, and the more positive our interpersonal relationships will be. Just try to put yourself in the mind of the one speaking and try to feel what they must be feeling and if you still do not agree with them, at least you would understand their point of view.

As the wise ones say,

"Wisdom is the reward you get for a lifetime of listening when you'd have preferred to talk."

Doug Larson

"Listening is a magnetic and strange thing, a creative force. The friends who listen to us are the ones we move toward. When we are listened to, it creates us, makes us unfold and expand."

Karl A. Menniger

"There is as much wisdom in listening as there is in speaking--and that goes for all relationships, not just romantic ones."

Daniel Dae Kim

"The most important thing in communication is hearing what isn't said"

Peter Drucker

"When people talk, listen completely. Most people never listen."

Ernest Hemingway

CHAPTER 7

Be Respectful and Helpful

Respect is one of those crazy English language words that can be used as both a noun and a verb. Because English is just plain confusing. However, both definitions essentially focus on having admiration and showing regard for the abilities, thoughts, feelings, qualities, traditions, and rights of others. Respect means that you recognize that your partner is a whole person and not just a way to get something that you want. It means that you know your partner has different experiences and opinions from you, and that's ok.

It's easy to *say* that you have respect for someone, but *acting* with respect can be a bit trickier.

Trust is essential in any relationship, even non-romantic ones. But it means a lot more than believing that your partner won't cheat on you, and *feeling* trust isn't nearly as powerful as *showing* that you trust your partner with your actions. Trust is the most major form of respect that you can show anyone and it shows that you respect their beliefs and thoughts and would appreciate and accept their decisions.

You can demonstrate trust by not texting or calling your partner constantly. Instead, text or call them once. Leave a message saying that you're thinking of them and that you hope to hear from them soon. This shows that you trust them to reach out to you when they can and that you know your partner appreciates your efforts.

This should go without saying, but don't go through your partner's phone or personal things without permission. If you have a weird feeling that they're trying to hide something from you, talk to them about it. There's no need to stir up drama if nothing is going on! It just feels disrespectful to sneak behind someone's back trying to uncover their secrets. You should have enough self-respect to demand the truth from them if you have suspicions. Which reminds me of my friend's boss and his wife. They were an elegant couple. Patricians at their finest. I was in awe of them actually and would gaze at them longingly whenever I visited my friend at the art gallery he worked at. The couple, Mr. and Mrs. Waldron, were usually there. Entertaining some aristocrats or reorganizing the art that they had just flown in from some extravagant place. They were a good-looking, sufficiently wealthy, and apparently happily married couple. Or so I thought. One day my friend told me to pick her up from the gallery and as I went in anticipating to see Mr. and Mrs. Waldron, I met a forbidding character at the entrance who wouldn't let me in until I called my friend to come out. She hurried out and dragged me with her to the car. "What's the matter?" I asked as we jumped into the car and I drove off. "It's a long story but the crux of the matter is, my bosses are splitting up." To say I was shocked would be an understatement. I couldn't comprehend it. It just did not make sense to me. I thought that they were totally compatible and perfectly happy together. But to my surprise, my friend told me that they had been having trouble trusting each other. Mrs. Waldron was tracing his cell phone and getting him followed. I gather that with money you have larger resources to give in to your suspicions and behave as erratically as you want. What she was doing is a classic case of utter disrespect and disregard for the other person's privacy and their feelings. She eventually realized that she had been misunderstanding the situation and Mr. Waldron was in fact, innocent. But before she gathered the courage to come clean, he had figured out the ugly truth and decided to divorce her. They are an original case of miscommunication and misconduct in marriage and I take a life lesson from their mistakes. I believe that Mr. Waldron had trouble listening to her complaints and did not address her issues in time which escalated into full-blown paranoia where she lost control of herself and acted impulsively, almost maniacally. The result is for everyone to see.

We need to stop taking our relationships for granted. All around me I see people not giving their relations their due respect. Whether it's their mother or brother or friend or neighbor, they would just not take enough time to listen to their requests and understand their feelings. Also, you cannot trust someone or give them your time until they are reliable. If they are constantly canceling on you and don't feel accountable for their poor choices, then you need to either have a talk with them and communicate your feelings clearly or maintain your distance, depending on how close you are with them. It goes with saying that you also need to follow through whenever *you're* the one making plans and requesting a meeting.

Don't say yes to dinner you're not sure you'll be able to go to. Instead, be accountable. Keep a calendar and check it when you and the other person are making plans. Don't say you'll call and then don't. Instead, set a reminder on your phone. Being dependable respects the time and emotional energy of other people. After all, it can be stressful to have your plans change constantly. But, there will be times when you wouldn't have a choice. Like an emergency or a delay at work. Then the respectable thing to do is to apologize. Say you're sorry, offer to reschedule, and make sure you check in with them when you're free.

One more way of giving respect is allowing the other person to choose to spend time with anyone they want. Your best friend must be pretty awesome and you would like her to give you company every day but, she might have other friends and family to spend time with and that's ok. You need to be able to respect her needs and give her some space. One of my colleagues was very sweet and she would try and go to lunch with me at the same time and at the same place where I ate every day so that she could have me as her company. But I wanted some quiet time too so I would try and brush her off on occasions. But, bless her heart, she couldn't take the clue and would try to join me daily. Things got so awkward, for me at least, that I started avoiding her at the office too just because I wanted her to get a signal. The more I ignored her the more she tried to please me by paying me compliments and seeking me out around the office to hand me a cup of coffee. I was very uncomfortable but then I realized that I was turning into this mean and nasty person and I went up to her and told her the truth. She would have got hurt at first but me not being honest with her was just doing her a disservice instead of saving her from embarrassment. At first, she stopped coming to lunch with me altogether but gradually we got into a routine where she accompanied me on alternate days and the rest of the days I would either eat alone or not take lunch at all. It allowed me the freedom to do as I wished while maintaining a balance between my workmate and me. The thing is, everyone needs a break from each other every once in a while. Spending time alone or with several different people means that both of you can continue to grow as individuals. You can both bring new ideas and activities to your relationship, keeping it exciting and engaging. It also gives you both a chance to talk about your relationship with your other friends or family members and get a fresh perspective on things.

The golden rule of giving respect is to appreciate each other's differences. Don't criticize your friend and daily member for their ideas or interests. You can disagree with someone and still respect their opinion. Part of what makes relationships awesome is the differences! Your partner, friend, or family member can help you see the world from a new perspective, even if you don't ultimately change your mind. You can show the other person you appreciate them by going to the events that are important to them like a seminar, a game, or an art show, even if you would never set foot in a baseball stadium or art gallery otherwise.

Accept their boundaries, even when they're different from yours. Don't pressure them into doing things that they don't want to even if they mean a lot to you. It's wrong to coerce them into an agreement and it's a wrong use of emotions and manipulation of their feelings for you. It's just plain disrespectful and it can damage your relationships in the long run.

Now it may seem difficult to show respect in relationships but it all comes down to being attentive and listening carefully to your loved ones and giving importance to their feelings.

It's as simple as hearing your partner, friend, or anyone you're close with and being kind to them. But, If your loved ones, especially your partner wants to know where you are all the time, frequently accuses you of lying or cheating, puts you down, calls you names, or is in any way physically aggressive, you may be in an abusive relationship. Abusive relationships are based on power and control, rather than respect. They take a serious toll on millions of people's lives each year. Even if your partner tells you that they do it out of love, there's always an underlying problem there that needs to be addressed.

Seeing a therapist or a counselor is highly recommended in case of any kind of abuse.

The compulsive need to be right all the time is the thing that ruins the respectful environment in a relationship. When people respect each other, they can accept not being right in favor of maintaining a healthy balance. People with successful relationships know how to choose their battles knowing that closeness means more than being right at times. The need to prove yourself right creates fear and resentment between people and will eventually wear the relationship down over time.

Relationships can be hard, I know. But, they can even be more difficult when you feel disrespected. When you start a relationship with a foundation of love and respect, you and your loved one can create a relationship that builds you both up to be stronger, happier, and more fulfilled. It all starts with respecting the other person and ends with communication and mutual understanding. As respect is crucial for all relationships. When you fail to respect the other person, you prevent yourself from getting honest respect from them in return. Your failure creates an environment where the other person can't be at their best. So, give respect to get respect and enjoy a fulfilling relationship with all the people that are close to your heart.

As you must have heard, a great relationship is about two things first, find out the similarities, and second respect the differences.

Communication and mutual understanding. As respect is crucial for all relationships. When you fail to respect the other person, you prevent yourself from getting honest respect from them in return. Your failure creates an environment where the other person can't be at their best.

So, give respect in order to get respect and enjoy a fulfilling relationship with all the people that are close to your heart. As you must have heard,

"Most good relationships are built on mutual trust and respect."

Mona Sutphen

"One of the most sincere forms of respect is actually listening to what another has to say."

Bryant H. McGill

"Respect commands itself and it can neither be given nor withheld when it is due."

Eldridge Cleaver

"Respecting someone indicates the quality of your personality."

Mohammad Rishad Sakhi

CHAPTER 8

Weigh Before You Speak

———◆———

Communication is key in a relationship. We've all heard this statement a million times but what to say and how to communicate your feelings is the most important aspect of communication. I always say I'm a great talker, but I have to also be an equally great listener in order to be a great communicator. You need to express yourself healthily and listen to the other person when they're doing the same and actually understanding the concepts and ideas that they need to impart is crucial to create two-way communication between any relationships. Now there are a few tips and tricks that need to be taken into account if you wish to establish a healthy communicating relationship.

The nonessentials of everyday life may take up most of your conversations but the real questions should go a little deeper. It's alright to ask about the other's day or talk about the weather but, it's about being able to dig deep and get to know this person as well as you can. It's not always easy to go above and beyond while interacting with certain people, especially for those who have never been comfortable talking about their feelings. And it's not necessary to make every conversation a heart-to-heart.

There are ways to do this without pressuring the other person to talk about their deepest thoughts. For example, instead of asking yes or no questions like "Did you have a good day at work?" try asking more open-ended questions like, "How was work?" Yes, they may respond with a brief and abrupt reply but asking open-ended questions allows them to share more if they choose to. Keep in mind that not everyone opens up very easily. Be patient with your loved ones if they are not sharing all the time. Here you'll need to show utmost respect and patience and really hone your listening skills if they should choose to share. Respect breeds trust which in turn breeds love and care. It's all interrelated really.

Now, if they reply to your question by saying, "My workday went okay...." but there is an underlying tension that can be identified in their words or you can feel a strong emotion in the undercurrents of their tone then that means that you need to pay more attention to it because there may be something else that they're feeling but not yet ready to communicate. Our tone and our attitude give away a lot more than just the words coming out of our mouths and it's honestly a skill to be able to pick up on those nonverbal signals.

Sometimes you can tell just by looking at someone what they may be feeling. It's not always easy to do this and let's face it: as much as we want to be mind readers, we aren't and shouldn't have to be. So, if you're not sure what your close relation is feeling, ask them.

If you're the one holding things in and expecting your loved one to read your mind, take a moment to appreciate the fact that your friend or family member is trying by asking you what's going on rather than ignoring the problem and not making an effort at all. Do your best to let them know how you're feeling when you're ready to open up about it. It's not healthy to say you're okay when you're not and then get mad at your partner for not figuring it out. Be honest about how you feel to the best of your ability and try to express it healthily before it gets to the point where it blows up and someone says something they regret. Remember, being direct is always better than being passive-aggressive.

There a certain words that need to be avoided in any kind of relationship. The first and foremost is the word, "should". If all your sentences include this word then your relationship is heading for problems. "You should be more considerate." "You should take me out at least twice a week." "You should be as nice as my BFF's boyfriend." "You should have given me a new bag for my birthday!"

All these statements act like landmines and would explode into arguments anytime soon. Also, this word, although spoken by most of us pretty casually, *SHOULD* be avoided. It actually makes your loved ones that they are not appreciated and their efforts are not appreciated by us. It's kind of demeaning if you think about it. Another word or rather a phrase that we need to avoid is "Why can't you be more like," This is also a damper. Never compare your partner, friend, or relation to someone else. Even if you think you're trying to help, this can carve a deep wound and leave a mark that you'll not be able to erase. Another one can be, "Why are you so, " Too often we fill in that blank with a negative word or statement that indicates what we see as a critical problem with our loved one. Yet the words are hardly accurate and are not as permanent as we deem at the time. They will only serve to make your relation feel less important and can hurt their egos. My favourite is, " I don't care, " I think we probably care a little too much to admit and just try to pretend that we are cool and unfazed. Not saying what you want and need is a successful way to make sure you don't get what you think you deserve. It's lying to yourself and is confusing for your loved ones. Also, don't comment on the physical looks but instead try to be an inspiration, "You've let yourself go" Demeaning comments about your partner's physical appearance are disrespectful and can put a real dent in your partner's confidence in themselves and the relationship itself. It can also make your loved one think that our relationship is conditional and dependent on their looks and dressing only. Lastly, "You're dumber than I thought!" Name-calling of any kind, even when done in a joking way, can express criticism and is a very hurtful and mean way to communicate.

The main thing to keep in mind would be that relationships have their ups and downs, and conversations can quickly develop into arguments with as little as one wrong word spoken in a moment of irritation. Protect yourself and your loved one from being offended by keeping the one most hurtful word out of your conversations with each other.

My friend's niece is a sweetheart. I adore her to bits and wish her the best in life. She practically grew up in front of me and is a genuine person. The only issue she has that she blathers a lot. I mean generally, she has to give a lot of input into a discussion, but she can say almost anything and some of the things she says may be deemed as politically incorrect. I consider her a kid although she became an adult last year, so I find it funny but her mother, who she lives with, finds it irritating to the point where it gets on her nerves. Jessica will bless her heart, never care about the consequences of her speech and it annoys people, mostly. One day it so happened, that Jessica was with her mom who was visiting a sick friend. The poor lady had caught some kind of virus that was supposed to be contagious. Now when Jessica and her mother arrived, they didn't have masks and they were told to put on the ones the lady's family handed out. All through the meeting, they were informed by the family of how deadly the virus could be and how swiftly it spread. Jessica was silent until the husband of the lady said that he wished it were him who had caught the virus instead of his wife because she was weak and fragile. Jessica instantly replied, "I wish so too!" the man started laughing and asked, "Why do *you* wish that it were *me?*" she replied, "so that we wouldn't have to come and see you and wouldn't be put at risk like this." All of them were still and you could hear the heavy breathing of the poor lady like a banging door. "Well, what she means is that *none* of you should have gotten this disease in the first place." Jessica's poor mother tried to cover up for her. "No mom! What are you saying? I meant I didn't want to come and visit so that *I* would not get sick!" Jessica replied and there was no saving face this time. Her mom quickly said her goodbyes and amid cold stares and unblinking glares, they left as soon as they could. Now what it shows is that Jessica may not have been trying to be mean and unkind but that is what it seemed like and probably broke the poor aunt's heart. This is not an example where it's a matter of life and death but it's a predicament we all go through sometimes and we need to think very carefully before speaking. What Jessica needs is to think before she speaks and keep from putting her foot in her mouth.

Many people are compelled to give voice to any passing feeling, thought, or impression they have. They randomly dump the contents of their mind without regard to the significance of what they are saying. When we talk about unimportant matters as gossiping about others, our attention is wasted on inconsequentialities.

One of my brother's ex-girlfriends had a habit of gossiping. A little bit of harmless gossip doesn't hurt but when it develops into an instinctual habit, someone should step in to halt the process. One day, they were hanging out in the backyard by the pool and all the rest of the family was inside. I was with my mom helping out in the kitchen. We were discussing my best friend's college application disaster and the girlfriend came into the kitchen to probably get a can of soda from the fridge. I was in the middle of the story and what she heard was, "applied to the college and got rejected 8 times! The institute must be used to receiving and rejecting the applications mom. What a loser!" Now my brother had also been rejected by a college recently, but he also got in a few and was just deciding on which one to join. His ex went back quietly, and I didn't even think anything of it until my brother came inside with a red face, glared at me in anger, and stormed off to his room. Now, my brother and I were pretty close, and I could sense that his behavior wasn't normal, so I went up to his room and saw him sitting on his bed still seething. I sat down next to him and spoke gently, "What's wrong? Are you mad at me for some reason?" he looked at me with a hurt look on his face and replied, "I am not a loser you know. One rejection doesn't make you a loser." I was very confused by his answer, so I demanded an explanation. "Yes. Of course, it doesn't. So, who said that?" and he looked at me indignantly. "Well, you did!" Now I was really lost. "I never said that! How can you blame me like this?" it was my turn to feel indignant. "Well, Stephanie said." And as he spoke her name, he realized his mistake and it dawned on him that his gossiping girlfriend had done it again but this time she had disrupted his feelings for his own sister who he knew would never say anything behind his back. He knew that If I wanted to call him a name I would do it to his face. I also remembered her sneaky entrance and exit from the kitchen earlier and told him what had happened. Needless to say, that a fight ensued, and she left with her bags packed. They didn't break up over that incident though so you cannot blame me for their separation. But she sure would have learned her lesson to not be such a gossip queen next time.

One of the strongest marks of ethical life is the art of correct speech. Perfecting our speaking technique is one of the main principles of mature people. Before talking take a few moments to contemplate what you will say and how you will say it while considering the impact they will have on the listener. Sweet words and kind statements are the reason for encouragement and a deeper connection for the people in your life and they appreciate your opinion, but I always say that honesty without tact is just cruelty. My friend's niece is a sweetheart. I adore her to bits and wish her the best in life. She practically grew up in front of me and is a genuine person. The only issue she has that she blathers a lot. I mean generally, she has to give a lot of input into a discussion, but she can say almost anything and some of the things she says may be deemed as politically incorrect. I consider her a kid although she became an adult last year, so I find it funny but her mother, who she lives with, finds it irritating to the point where it gets on her nerves. Jessica will bless her heart, never care about the consequences of her speech and it annoys people, mostly. One day it so happened, that Jessica was with her mom who was visiting a sick friend. The poor lady had caught some kind of virus that was supposed to be contagious. Now when Jessica and her mother arrived, they didn't have masks and they were told to put on the ones the lady's family handed out. All through the meeting, they were informed by the family of how deadly the virus could be and how swiftly it spread.

Jessica was silent until the husband of the lady said that he wished it was him who had caught the virus instead of his wife because she was weak and fragile. Jessica instantly replied, "I wish so too!" the man started laughing and asked, "Why do *you* wish that it was *me?*" she replied, "so that we wouldn't have to come and see you and wouldn't be put at risk like this." All of them were still and you could hear the heavy breathing of the poor lady like a drum banging.

You may want to talk about something light and fun and share an enjoyable experience or you may need to discuss something very serious and grave. The point is to do it lovingly and keep an open mind while listening to the other's thoughts. When you need to talk bluntly about something difficult with another person, you must focus on the conversation with acute concentration and purpose. During the chat, you must listen patiently, speak tactfully, and tell the truth as you understand it. You should associate your words, variation of expression and tone, eye gestures, body language, and actions with your inner awareness in an honest discussion. Another thing that you must focus on is, apologizing for your mistakes. To avoid pain and stress in any relationship you should be mindful to express your remorse in a clear and friendly way so that the other person can get over their bad feelings and the discussion can move forward. By acknowledging that you were wrong, discussing what is allowed and not allowed in your relationship, expressing your regret and remorse, learning from your mistakes, and find new ways of dealing with difficult situations, opening up a line of communication with the other person.

A sincere apology can cause a great sense of relief especially if you have guilt over your words or actions. But you have to keep in mind that an apology alone doesn't erase the hurt or make everything alright, it does show that you know your actions or words were wrong and that you will strive harder in the future to prevent it from happening again.

Not apologizing when you are wrong can be damaging to your personal and professional relationships. It can also lead to cogitation, anger, resentment, and hostility that may only cultivate over time. If what you did would have bothered you if it were done to you, an apology is clearly in order. If you're not sure, an apology offers you the chance to "own" mistakes you made but re-establish what you think was okay. If you feel the other person is being unreasonable, a discussion may be in order. You can decide where you stand on the apology after that. The main thing is to voice your concerns whether they are regarding your behavior or your loved ones'.

Saying something vague like, "I'm sorry if you were upset by something I said," implies that the hurt feelings were an arbitrary response on the part of the other person. But saying, "When I said the thing that I said, I wasn't thinking. I realize I hurt your feelings, and I'm sorry," shows that you know what it was you said that hurt the other person, and you take responsibility for it.

Don't make assumptions and don't try to blame it on others. Speak clearly and concisely that you are truly sorry and will not do or say it again. This will also encourage the other person to come forward and take responsibility for their actions and decisions. Discussing what type of rules, you both will adhere to in the future will rebuild trust and positive feelings in the relationship.

Discussions are not always easy, but that can be an important part of mending or maintaining important relationships. With empathy, an open heart, and a dose of courage, you can take the steps you need to create a sincere and honest environment for expressing yourself. I love these sayings by a dynamic women.

"We are stronger when we listen, and smarter when we share."

Rania Al-Abdullah

"Your words will either give you joy or give you sorrow, but if they were spoken without regret, they give you peace."

Shannon Alder

"There is no communication that is so simple that it cannot be misunderstood."

Luigina Sgarro

CHAPTER 9

Emotional Well-Being in Relationships

Our emotional health is an inherent part of our life and maintaining healthy relationships. Upholding good emotional health is all about our ability to manage and control our emotions and building up pliability when we face rough times. While positive emotions are necessary and indicate a healthy emotional self, it doesn't necessarily mean that you only be happy all the time. Emotional well-being lets your relationships become healthier and more positive. Experiencing good relationships with others may be the single most important source of life satisfaction and emotional well-being. Supportive relations are related to good health, including emotional health, because they are protective factors against stress and problems. Emotionally healthy relationships can happen with anyone in our lives, from romantic partners to family members to friends to coworkers or others with whom we socialize regularly. Emotionally healthy relationships are the kind of relationships in our lives that are positive and boost both parties. Such relationships make people feel glad for the connection and you can start depending on the person with whom you have a healthy link.

So, what are emotional health and mental well-being? Emotional and mental health are intrinsically linked, and the terms are often used in place of each other. However, there are a few vital differences. There is a clear association between wellbeing, good mental health, and improved outcomes for people of all ages and social classes across a whole bunch of areas. Enhanced wellbeing is linked to longevity, physical health, and social connectedness, educational achievement, maintaining a home, employment status, and productivity.

The best way to think about it is that mental health and emotional wellbeing are a bit like a team, you can't have one without the other. Mental health refers to the way we process information. It is to do with the cognitive way the brain understands situations, this can be diminished by chemical imbalances caused by mental illness, such as depression. On the other hand, emotional health refers to how we deal with and express our feelings. If your mental health is suffering, it's likely that your ability to normalize your emotions will be worn-out, so it's important to consider both when it comes to your overall happiness and comfort. Strong evidence exists to show a link between wellbeing and having a sense of purpose and meaning in daily life. Purpose and meaning can come from many sources, including family and friends, social inclusion, leisure, creativity, community involvement, and spirituality. Developing an attitude of purpose and meaning assists us in the development of positive self-esteem, personal growth, lower stress levels, greater resilience, and positive emotions, and eventually, better relationships.

Now the next part to focus on is how to take care of your emotions and mental health. It's common knowledge that looking after your mental health will have long-lasting advantages for your quality of life. The way we function as individuals influences every aspect of our lives. Not just the personal stuff, but also relationships, family, and work.

The same is also true for your emotional health. As our mind, body, and emotions are so basically interconnected, there is a positive cumulative effect when you take care of at least one of these areas. For example, there are evident physical benefits of investing in your emotional health. According to researchers, if you're emotionally vulnerable and feel depressed, it has a negative effect on your immune system that can lead to many illnesses. If you are suffering from stress, anxiety, or other emotional negativity, you can experience exhaustion and lack of energy which can lead to tensions in a relationship.

When you're confident in managing and expressing your own feelings, it allows you to be more compassionate towards others. Whether it's a friendship or a romantic relationship, you'll be able to connect on a deeper level. This ability to communicate your feelings will also help you navigate disagreements and hold your own in arguments, this could help you evade toxic relationships with emotionally controlling people.

Our emotional health also aids to create a good relationship with ourselves. Your self-esteem can be majorly affected if you're struggling to cope with stress or if negative thoughts are taking over your mind. If you've invested in your emotional wellbeing and have built up strength, you will be able to see the good in yourself in spite of the trials you are facing around you.

Now, what are the steps that you need to take in order to improve your emotional and mental health? I will discuss a few important ones here.

Taking care of yourself is one of the most important parts of sustaining good emotional wellbeing. Although self-care can mean different things to different people, there is some nitty-gritty that will help anyone feel better about themselves. Sleep is a huge part of caring for one's self. We should all be trying to get at least 8 hours of shut-eye per night and try to relax as much as we can before getting to bed. Sleep deprivation is known to reduce our emotional flexibility, making it tougher to process our feelings and more receptive to negativity. Additionally, resting and maintaining a good sleeping cycle, a healthy diet, and regular workouts also help you self-improve and enhance self-love. While it is alright to enjoy and indulge yourself once in bloom, you need to create a routine for yourself to follow. Man is a creature of routine and as much as we enjoy our late nights and sleeping in, we thrive when we set up a time for everything. Cooking is also a therapeutic process and by cutting, slicing, frying, or baking nutritional food for ourselves, we go into a meditational mode and it helps us relax and appreciate ourselves more. Eating healthy and taking the time to work out a few days a week means you're looking after yourself which in turn helps you establish a healthy lifestyle and better emotional persona.

If you're undergoing negative emotions, suppressing them will only make you feel worse. Sometimes it can be tempting to bury our heads in the sand and ignore how we're feeling, and, in some cases, it can be difficult to voice our concerns or anxieties, as that will make them come to life and you'll have to acknowledge their existence once they are out in the open. Yet, not only will bottling up these negative sentiments influence your emotional wellbeing, but they could also lead to more serious mental or physical health issues.

Opening up to your friends and family can also help reduce feelings of isolation and loneliness which are two of the biggest hurdles to reaching your desired emotional health. Part of being emotionally healthy is knowing when to ask for help and support. If this is something you find hard to do, a therapist or counselor may be able to help you get more comfortable with being more open about your thoughts and feelings.

As I said earlier, being emotionally healthy isn't about being happy all the time. But there is a lot to be said for trying to identify the positive parts of life. This doesn't have to be reserved for special occasions or going on holidays. You can find gratitude every day by being glad that you got a seat on the train or that the meeting you were worried about went well or your friend or family took the time to sit and eat with you. Taking the time to notice these little things will help you feel more positive about your situation in life overall, even when experiencing stressful circumstances.

A good way to practice gratitude is to start writing a journal that you fill out at the end of each day. The act of physically writing down your small triumphs and dedicating a set amount of time to positive thoughts will help you finish the day on a happy, healthy note. Positive affirmations are becoming a common practice nowadays and it seems to be helping a lot of people find their space and happy zone.

You'll also need to work on your abilities to cope with transition and pressure, emotional understanding, and skills to regulate emotions, stress reduction and relaxation skills, taking part in meaningful activities, good physical health, including diet, exercise, healthy use of alcohol and other drugs, positive interactions with family and social network contacts, and steady participation in social and community life.

You'll notice there are a lot of social aspects to the mentioned steps. Active participation in social and community life is strongly linked to mental health and well-being. It is also important in maintaining resilience during times of stress for the development of your relationships.

So the story that I am going to tell you is about me. When I was in college, I carried a feeling of heaviness with me. I was struggling with self-esteem issues and I found it difficult to communicate my emotions with my friends and family members. I didn't know how to talk about it because I had not accepted my situation myself. It was an awfully low point of my life and I still feel the pang of sadness whenever I recall it. The change of environment and location had further impacted my morale and I further constrained myself into a shell. It was an excruciatingly unhappy experience and I do not wish it on anyone. My mom would worry about it because she's a mother and has a natural, built-in instinct to sense for something that bothers her children but she also didn't know how to help me. Mainly because I didn't open up about it and never bared my soul in front of her. If I had, I am sure she would have made everything better because she's my closest friend and my confidant. But at the time I was stupidly internalizing my emotions which was hurting me more.

One day, I was invited to a party on campus and like always I refused to go. I usually would entertain myself by going down to the auditorium and helping out with the arts and painting of the backgrounds for plays and musicals. But on that particular day, I was happy because I had scored an A on my test. So I decided to attend the party on a whim. It was a teacher and student event and everyone I knew was present. I suddenly became shy and felt an outbreak of self-consciousness that was very common for me. But this time it was a crippling sense of being a loser that I just could not shake. My mouth felt dry and I had difficulty swallowing. I was standing in a corner contemplating to make a smooth exit when one of my teachers approached and called out my name. I jumped in surprise and turned to see my English literature professor holding out a glass of punch in one hand and sporting a big grin. "I love your work! You should help out with the art supplies unit more often. I will give you extra credit for it too!" he said and I was flabbergasted. My face turned beet red and I stammered an unclear thank you. Then someone handed me a henna cone and pushed me towards a bunch of giggling girls who were shoving their hands in my face existing me to draw designs on them. I sat down and began making patterns on their hands and loved every minute of it. The girls, some of whom took classes with me, were very friendly and they honestly didn't notice me in the class at all. I made new friends that day but most importantly I realized that the problem wasn't with anyone else, it was with me. I had been self-conscious and people thought it best to let me be. I also let a few guys at the party afterward and they all previously thought that I was arrogant and had a very standoffish attitude. I was shocked to hear that! I had never in my life thought this way about myself and had live in fear of being rejected and ridiculed by everyone. It's pretty sad, I know. Nonetheless, I learned my lesson and relaxed a little bit. The main thing is that everyone should be comfortable in their own skin. It doesn't matter who you are, what you look like, and where you come from. If you live yourself and take care of yourself then you will build the basis of every relationship on honesty and sincerity. If you care about yourself, then you will definitely care about other people around you. Therefore, it's crucial to develop a solid mental foundation and protect your emotional self. Think of it as meditation or praying which help you reach a level of peace and serenity. Just like someone clever once said,

"Relationships can't blossom unless there is meaningful communication. That's why 'supplication is the key to worship.' It is a sign of meaningful communication between God and a person."

Suhaib Webb

CHAPTER 10

Be Clear and Honest

The truth can be uncomfortable, but a couple that has mutual respect is one that isn't afraid to put it out there. They can deal with the feelings of anger that might come from discussing harsh truths because they have the bigger picture in mind. If you want respect, then don't be scared of the truth. Honesty in a relationship is extremely important because it is the fundamental thing that makes a person feel safe. Even if you think the truth will be hard for your partner to hear, they will appreciate it in the long run. There are many traits that you must have to keep a healthy relationship with your partner, friend, or family member but honestly is required in *every* relationship full-time. You have no relationship if there is no honesty between you and the other person. Each lie that your loved one catches you in weakens your friendship, turning you from partners and confidants to adversaries in an unseen clash where your word is never taken seriously and why should it be? If you consort to lies in your daily routine and there is an evasive answer in almost all of your declarations, then there should not be any need for anyone to trust you again. But on the other hand, as I have said before, honesty without tact is just cruelty. So you need to keep in mind that you need to use subtlety when trying to explain your point. Speaking the truth and being clear about your feelings is the most important aspect of a relationship but you need to be extremely careful and gentle. There is no need to be brutal when delivering your opinion or answering questions honestly that you know might hurt. If your mom does your laundry for you sometimes but you see that the ironing is all creased. What do you think you should say? Should you point it out to her in a hurtful way, say it in casual tones, or not say anything at all? I suggest that you mention it in the passing while also thanking her for the effort and time she spent on you. If you say, "You always do a bad job ironing my clothes!" that is just plain rude. If you stay quiet about it, it will develop into a chronic problem that will irritate you endlessly and your mom would have no idea that you feel this way and all her hard work will go to waste. Just add a sentence in a conversation with your mom and say, "Hey! By the way, thank you so much for doing my laundry mom. I really appreciate it. It's just that I think it becomes very tiring for you because some of my shirts were all creased so, please if it's too much work for you then let me know and I will do it myself. Thanks!" This will show her that you are grateful for her actions but you want to make a few minor modifications to the favour.

Honesty in a relationship means always telling your companion, no matter who that may be, the truth, and being totally open with them, both for the substantial things and the minor things. If you're avoiding talking to your loved one about something, such as things that are bothering you in the relationship, something you did that you know your partner will be upset about, or how you really feel about the things you talk about together, then you aren't being honest. Being honest means being your true self around your friend and family member, never hiding who you are, what you think, or how you feel. This reminds me of another story. So my best friend and her husband are a cure couple. They are adorable and sweet and very much in love with each other but being her best friend, I know that my friend cannot cook to save her life! She is the worst chef there is but she doesn't notice it when people don't eat her food. Also, she loves cooking. So, it's a dilemma and I feel sorry for her husband. As much as I love her, I can't seem to gather enough courage to tell her and thankfully I don't have to endure it every day. But the poor guy has to go through the ordeal daily because she insists on preparing food for him. You might think that she would get better after doing it every day but no, she has not. If anything, her cooking skills have become worse! Anyways, one day both of them were invited for dinner at my place and Stacy went into the kitchen to help warm up the food. Her husband found the opportunity to confide in me that he had no idea how to tell her. "I don't want to hurt her feelings but it's a nightmare that I sit through every lunch and dinner time." Especially now, during the pandemic, when everyone is working from home. "I insist on cooking myself or taking her out for most of the days but she just doesn't relent," he tells me miserably and I understand completely. My advice to him was to let her down gently. Just add it in the passing and smile to let her know that it's alright.

They went home that night and I don't know what happened but Stacy called me in the morning and complained about her husband's rude comments. I was waiting for this moment and had prepared my speech. " Stace, you know the I love you. But Oliver is right, although you put your heart and soul into the food you make it just doesn't taste the way you want it to taste. I am sorry. Maybe you could take a cooking class or try your hand at baking instead?" I am sure she was shocked but she took it well and actually took my suggestions seriously. They both worked their problems out, no matter how small they were, and now live a happy, guilt-free life and I am so happy for them. All they needed was a little bit of honesty to make everything better.

What you don't want to do is to overshare or expect your loved one to tell you every teeny bit of detail. Sometimes people can get a little wrapped up in trying to make sure they know absolutely everything about each other. For example, someone might insist on sharing an email address or knowing exactly where their friend or spouse is at all times, or they might feel entitled to tell their loved one how better they think other people's relationships are, even if the comments may hurt their feelings.

It is necessary to understand the difference between secrets and privacy. Think of it this way, privacy is a barrier protecting your own thoughts, ideas, emotions, and past experiences that don't directly impact the people around you. A secret is something deceitful in a way and deliberately kept hidden from them for fear of creating the wrong perception of you and to avoid retribution. The best way to judge yourself is to look deep into your heart and find out if there is something that you are intentionally avoiding to tell your closest relationships because you are afraid of their reaction. Then you are hiding a secret but if there is nothing serious that you think you should tell them and still if the topic gets started and you are asked a direct question, then you need to speak up and be clear about your views. That was a private thought but it got shared because you have nothing to hide it be ashamed of. You don't have to tell the other person almost everything about yourself but if the need arises then transparency is the best policy.

Another thing to remember is, mean what you say. If you tell everyone that you are a punctual person but reach late everywhere, then your commitment will be considered mere empty words and no one will take you seriously. Building trust happens through actions, not just words so, show up when you say you will. Do the things you promise. Nothing wears out trust and builds resentment certainly like empty or broken promises. Most people avoid saying no to save others' feelings from getting hurt. I say, Better to be honest now and disappoint a little at the moment than disappoint later and destroy the trust. Once you establish communicating with each other an open priority in your relationship, having a conversation and agreeing that you'll both be open with each other about how you're feeling, what you need, what's working, and what's not, will make life much easier for you. By establishing this exemplary module, you make honesty effortless to practice for both of you. Getting someone to open up also requires tons of patience. Set a precedent for being honest and clear about your likes and dislikes and your loved one would mimic the same. They will see the advantages of becoming straightforward and would want the same for themselves. Tell them how you're feeling or what you're up to, and allow them to follow your lead. When your partner, friend, or family member sees that you're always being real with them, they'll feel like it's safe for them to be genuine with you.

Create a space for your loved one to become more open and honest with you. If you shoot someone down as soon as they let their guard down, then they will most likely never open up their hearts to you again. Even if you feel attacked by their accusations and you get hurt by their words. Appreciate them for their sincere opinions and let them know the truth in return, which is that you felt hurt by their words. Discussing it rather than keeping it inside will damage your mental health and then your relationships. Work on finding ways to feel safe and secure in your correlation. Committing repeatedly to being totally honest with each other will be an important first step to a healthy and non-toxic association with anyone.

CHAPTER 11

Have Empathy

Empathy is the skill to emotionally comprehend what other people feel, observe things from their point of view, and visualize yourself in their place. Basically, it is putting yourself in someone else's situation and feeling what they must be feeling. When you see another person undergoing difficulties, you would be able to imagine yourself in the other person's place and feel sympathy for what they must be going through.

What's the difference between empathy and sympathy when you are paying attention to someone else? The Webster dictionary defines empathy as "the action of understanding, being aware of, being sensitive to, and vicariously experiencing the feelings, thoughts, and experience of another…" The definition of sympathy includes "inclination to think or feel alike: emotional or intellectual accord…the act or capacity of entering into or sharing the feelings or interests of another…" Not a huge difference between the two, right?

Empathy can be best defined as an emotion to have genuine care about another person.

Empathy is not permission or acceptance. It is merely understanding, the instinctive sensing of another person's basic sentiments, needs, and psychological dynamics, practically looking at the world from behind the other's eyes. Asking yourself, how should I be feeling if I were him or her?

Now like all the skills mentioned above, empathy can be practiced until you get better at it.

Empathy is something that you can teach your kids and start a routine at home with your family. The more you instil it among your loved ones the more they are likely to exercise it with others and so on. To have a healthy and strong relationship, it's important for you and your friend or family member to feel strongly linked with each other. Empathy develops emotional bond and strength in all of our relationships and there is no sincerity between two people if they don't empathize with each other. Being empathetic implies that you are aware of someone's perceptions from their standpoint and you feel what they sense. While it is significant to be compassionate in every personal relationship you uphold, empathy is particularly important to maintaining a long-lasting relationship with your partner or spouse. You need to experience the feeling of being understood and heard which make a great way to feel like you and your partner a better team. You need to work harder on a connection with your partner or spouse because this is a relation based on love and respect. All the other relationships, apart from friendships, are god-gifted, and for you to maintain them for life, you need to put in extra efforts and commit to the love you have proclaimed.

That being said, empathy is most commonly seen between parents and their children. Old age can slow you down and some people specifically suffer from illnesses and other indispositions.

Less empathetic people tend to lack an awareness of how they truly feel in contrasting circumstances. Therefore, a reasonable starting point is to refresh the memory of people to assess how they really feel as they withstand life's good, bad, and neutral experiences. They need to be ready for a curveball whenever they are thrown one and analyze their own thoughts about the happenings. This drill will make way for neural networks which will be strengthened over time, to allow for a person to understand the experience, first their own, then that of others.

I place my bets on communication once again. Anyone happy in a relationship, either romantic or platonic, often show their empathy by communicating using words and expressions and letting the other person know that they are taking the time to imagine what they may be going through. The main thing is to pay attention to the *emotions* the other person is feeling rather than focusing on beliefs, ideas, rights, and wrongs of the situation. Keeping an open mind to illuminate others' sentiments is what empathy is all about. Of course, it needs patience and composure to provide all your attention to the other person and listen to their story. An empathetic person would listen attentively and aim to get a sense of the internal feelings such as hurt, fear, or shame that are usually behind anger or a tough exterior. A real friendship and companion involves evolving and maturing together with time. This suggests helping each other out when they need it most, without judging the other person and making them feel insignificant.

My mother's younger brother, uncle George was not. Much older than me and thus we became good friends and confidants when I grew up a little and moved out of my parents' house. Now as much as I loved my uncle, he was a little pompous for my taste. I would be telling him about my bargaining skills at the flea market and he would begin lecturing me on the ethical rights of a producer and seller. I would talk about the Indian place across the road and he would explain to me the health hazards I had faced by visiting the restaurant. It was fine with me because as we all know, everyone possesses a larger forgiving tendency when it comes to the family. Anyway, cutting the long story short, Uncle George got a girlfriend. She was a very sweet-natured person and I immediately hit it off with her. We hung out a lot over weekends because I rented a studio apartment close to their place. I started noticing signs of trouble after a few months and things escalated quickly after that. Miranda and I had become friends by then and she would sometimes open her heart up to me but of course, there was an unsaid agreement between us about my uncle. We never discussed him as that would create awkwardness between us. But, one day she couldn't control it anymore and came to my apartment. I opened the door to her teary-eyed face and knew immediately that something was seriously wrong. I ushered her in and she started unraveling her side of the story. It looked like uncle George was a fine specimen of modern-day youth but he lacked compassion and empathy where he had been enriched with ethics and know-how of rights of others. Simply put, he lacked empathy. He would strive so hard to be politically correct all the time that he did not pause to take in the sentiments behind an act or a statement. She told me that she felt like she had been living with a morally just robot. Who knew the rights and wrongs and always did the ethically proper thing bit had little to show in the name of compassion, and tenderness of heart. He would listen attentively and did not sabotage the other person's argument but did not feel the emotions on a deeper level. She felt disconnected from him and did not know how to bridge the gap between them. The main problem was that he did not know that he was lacking in anything and needed to work on himself. He was just stupefied when Miranda got frustrated with him one day and completely blew up. He wasn't expecting an outburst when according to him there was an issue, to begin with. Well, it goes to show that listening attentively without actually feeling the emotions of the other person may result in unnecessary and unintentional friction between relationships.

Being more in tune with your partner's sensitivities and feelings can enable you to observe when they are quiet and down before they even hint at anything. When you begin to ask questions about their emotional condition, it can demonstrate that you are involved in their contentment and invested in the relationship. Some couples struggle with being empathetic toward one another because having empathy is a relationship skill that not everyone has been acquainted with, or has taken the time to acquire and make an essential part of life.

Miranda came from an underprivileged home and had to struggle all her life for basic needs. Her parents tried their best to provide but they needed to cut down on extra expenses just so they could make the ends meet. It was all fine and most of us come from such backgrounds but the thing was that she was specifically against wasting anything. Uncle George was ok with it and they had a routine set up to accommodate her preferences. She hated using plastics or didn't purchase things in foam containers. She wasn't a minimalist, she just endorsed no waste policy. I personally think that it is awesome and we all should exercise this at home. Anyway, whenever they went out to eat, Miranda gets strongly about not going to ultra-luxurious places, she was more sensible in spending money and tried to look for options that offered better value for their money. That also wasn't an issue with Uncle George, it just wasn't up for discussion. He didn't understand the depth of Miranda's feelings and usually overlooked it as just practicality. This bothered her very much and whenever she tried to communicate her feelings, he would just shut her down. It grew into other aspects of their lives and his self-righteousness would distract him from the main point. For instance, at a friend's house warming party, Miranda wanted to make something at home, which would have taken days, and gift her but George saw it as a form of being a cheapskate and reminded her that the particular friend had gifted them something expensive on a birthday. Well, he wasn't wrong but he did not understand Miranda's point of view. She was putting her effort and love into the gift and also wanted to save a few bucks. She good me that they had finally had a full-fledged fight and she had moved out. It was caused by all the pent-up emotions and misunderstandings between them and she asked if she could stay at my place for a couple of days until she figured out her living situation. I agreed and let her be for the day and then called Uncle George and did my best to explain to him how Miranda felt. He came over, apologized for being an ape and they got together again. I am glad that this ended well but most of us have no common person who can make us see the truth and work towards reconciliation. Most of us just part ways instead of resolving our communication issues.

Real understanding calls for maturing and learning together. That implies supporting each other when they require it the most, without judging the other person and making them feel insignificant. These people can abstain from making judgments of their spouse's, friends, or family member's preferences and deduce that those selections were made after cautious reflection, regardless of whether or not they finally lead to happiness. Thinking that their loved ones are decent and ingenious people lays the basis for all promising and favourable relations.

Another great practice to exercise empathy is to adopt some of your loved one's duties from day-to-day life just to see what they put up with every day. It can help you understand what they go through on the daily basis and can help you stop being judgemental. Having empathy, or the ability to look past your own opinion, to that of a friend or family member, encourages you when making decisions because it allows for serious concern for your relative's or friend's needs and wants before an action.

But, there is a small problem with being empathic all the time, which is that it can become mentally exhausting. The emotions of others might come to be your emotions, too. So, try to show more compassion in your relationship to help relieve this. There is a way to still show empathy without losing your unique perspective of what you may feel in any given situation.

We cannot be more sensitive to pleasure without being more sensitive to pain ~Alan Watts

Friends and Family

The Importance of family values and friendship is common knowledge around the world in every culture and society. A lot of people aim to create a family and having friends is typical for every person. All of us believe these two factors the most important in our lives. Let's find out why!

In the olden times, there was a tradition that people would be gathered in groups that were called clans. All fellows of the clan helped each other and called each other kin or relatives. Important decisions and mutual grief was taken care of and there was an incredible ability to trust one another and believe in the sincerity of everyone.

Nowadays, it's the same concept even though the human race had grown exponentially. We can still do about anything for our family and the live affection occurs naturally. The role of the family in a person's life is very substantial. The magnitude of this component cannot be made too much of. All we do is for our family and all we have left in the end are the people who love us and who we love as much. So why not establish good communicating skills to help further build our relationships and engage with our loved ones more. As the say,

"Communication is the first pillar of love."

Alan Maiccon

1: Your Parents

They say you don't know pain until you crave a conversation with someone who is no longer alive. The most unfortunate and tragic situation you can encounter in life is the loss of a loved one. Now there's no sequence to death, anyone may depart anytime but realistically speaking and looking at the statistics of the world, older people tend to depart this world first. Personally, I don't want to think about my patents' demise but it may be a reality in the near future. We can not foresee or predict but we *can* control the time we have with them and spend it most positively and healthily.

Our parents, closest to us since birth and throughout life, support us because we are their family. Every one of us recognizes and associates with them from childhood. Parents teach us everything they know themselves: thanks to them, we can walk, talk, eat, read and write. If we never had them who would we be now? From the day we are born till the day they are with us, they become our support systems, whether it be emotional, financial, or psychological. We owe them everything. It doesn't matter how old you are, whatever you do, no matter who you have become, your parents will always assist and comfort you.

Unfortunately, not everyone can gloat about having good relations with their parents, and sometimes they cannot get backing from them. There can be many reasons for this like misunderstandings, disagreements, differences of opinion. Nevertheless, it is absolutely critical to make the utmost efforts to get close to them. Sometimes it is very difficult, due to physical and emotional distances but it's never too late to ask for forgiveness or explain your point of view so that you are understood and appreciated.

You need to do everything in your power to mend the most important and fundamental relationship you have. Nothing is too much when it comes to your parents. In some cultures, parents have been deemed the next best thing on earth to God and there is a verse that tells you not to even cluck your tongue at them in frustration.

My mother is one of the most loving, caring, and interfering people I know. I say this not as a joke. She truly is a force to be reckoned with and wouldn't let up if she makes up her mind about something. She would badger you until you conceded and did as she told you. All of this is out of love and none of us feel smothered by her affection as youngsters these days would like to call it. She is my rock and my favourite person in the whole world. But, there comes a time when we don't see eye to eye and that's ok. I will always be able to count on her no matter what happens and am assured by her presence. We debated over my college selection, argued when I moved out, disagreed about my first job, and have been having unresolved issues to this day. Yet, she is the one I will go to when I need guidance, she is the one with all the answers, and she is the one I have the deepest connection with. We constantly communicate our feelings and our relationship grows stronger every day. You need to trust your parents' vision and their experiences. You may feel, like me, that your parents are overpowering and they dominate your life most of the time but you need to trust in them because no matter how much they meddle they will always want the best for you.

Remember, apart from a few exceptions, no one can be more dependable, honest, and sincere with you than your parents. They have the knowledge and wisdom to guide you and subjugate your fears and insecurities. They will be the happiest at your success and heartbroken at your loss. They are connected to you in such a unique and divine way and that no other relationship can replace them. They are truly a God's gift to mankind.

2: Your Partner

I believe that your partner is the next most important person in your life after your parents. I may be biased, but I think that your children, as much as you love them, come after your partner. At least, in my opinion, that should be the case with everyone. Your partner can be your spouse, boyfriend, or someone with who you are romantically involved with. This relationship is the basis of all the other relationships to come. This is who you opt for in life and decide to spend a good amount of time with them if not your whole life. We choose our partners depending on their personalities and the understanding that we develop with them and vice versa.

The significance of our relationship is demonstrated by the term "Better halves" which means that our spouse is a part of us and that too, the one making us a better person.

Sometimes we as couples can feel discontented, unhappy, and disappointed in our marriages or romantic relationships and have no idea what exactly is wrong. There can be many reasons that partake in a happy and satisfied relationship some of them are love, commitment, trust, attention, open communication the essentials of which are mentioned above as listening, tolerance, patience, honesty, respect, sharing, forgiveness, etc. But, it's easier said than done. Many couples struggle with the most basic rules of a relationship and they battle with each other over creating a healthy balance. I see so many friends and family members who are living miserable lives with their partners and are toiling with the idea of improvement. The simple fact is, if you are unhappy at home you will be unhappy outside of your home too. Your work, business, friendships, and other associations will suffer subsequently. People around you will recognize your sadness and will be affected by your dissatisfaction and let me tell you a secret, no one wants to mingle with a downer. People socialize to lift their moods and have a good time. There are rare occasions when people discuss their problems and seek advice from friends but those are uncommon. Mostly, people want to enjoy themselves and they rarely like to associate with someone who is constantly dampening their spirits with sadness and despair.

My advice to the people who love each other and live together but still don't seem to get along well would be to get closer. It is important that couples spend as much time together as they can. With busy schedules, multiple commitments, or children to care for couples can find themselves with very little time for each other. By spending time together regularly, like shopping, dining out, going to the movies, walking, swimming, playing sports, exercising, sharing other hobbies, and going on holidays can help couples become closer and have more time to talk to each other. Therefore they get to know one another better and acquire a better understanding of the other person. Once couples get to know and understand each other more deeply and also beget empathy for each other, it helps them get closer emotionally as well. Emotional closeness involves being open with each other about your feelings, beliefs, values, hopes, thoughts, worries, fears, dreams, and ambitions.

Also, for a couple, it is crucial to be close physically. This can entail eye contact, holding hands, hugging, snuggling, massaging one another, etc. Bodily closeness can hugely augment a couple's sense of closeness and intimacy. It is vital for couples to be aware that some people are more comfortable being physically expressive than others and it is important to try to understand how comfortable or contrarily your partner feels and take it from there. This can lead to another kind of closeness which is only possible between romantically involved partners. It is important that both the partners are happy with their sexual relationship and feel able to raise and discuss their sexual needs with the other as desired. Sometimes it so happens that couples can be very concerned about the frequency of their sexual activity. That being said, it is all a personal preference but an essential component to build a healthy and stable love life.

3: Your Children

I personally think that the people you most love in life are your kids. There is no match for the love and affection you have for them and rightly so because there is no one more intrinsically connected to you than the babies you give birth to. They are genetically linked to you in the most primal way and no matter what you do or what they do, they will never be far away from your thoughts.

A capability to form and maintain relationships is necessary to us and how we behave within society. It is the main element to being mentally healthy and having a positive awareness of wellbeing. This is valid for children and young people of all ages as well, from the very early years through the teenage years, they need the sense of belonging as much as us adults. In the initial years of a baby's life, the brain is developing and it is at its most adaptable during these years. So, the way we communicate and interact with the child can be fundamental for their healthy mental and emotional development. Children who are secure and have the comfort of living in a happy household with their parents turn out to be emotionally stable and strong. The ones who are attached and grounded by their loved ones are better able to manage their own feelings and behaviours and can sufficiently relate to others. The youngsters get off to a good start in terms of their social development as well. As they grow, their ability to forge and nurture relationships with their schoolmates, parents, teachers, co-workers, and partners develops further.

Unfortunately, kids with learning disabilities have a tough time forming relationships with others but it is not limited to a handicap the kids are born with, sometimes the incapability emerges from abnormal parenting and childhood traumas. This, we need gentle discipline and unconditional love and support to raise our kids right, for the sake of our relationship with them and their relationship with the world. If a parent is stressed, it will surely impact the child. If there is a case of bullying, the child will suffer internally and may resort to self-harm. It is difficult for kids to regulate their emotions and deal with stressful situations but it's the caregiver or guardian's job to help them understand their feelings and vent off the unnecessary, pent-up sentiments. Relationships are important on so many levels, and across the course of life. But, if we can make sure that children and young adults can establish and retain positive relationships in ways that are accepted by them, then this will help get them off to a good start in life and aid their mental development. Your extended family can also give emotional and physical support if required. Grandparents, aunties, uncles, and cousins actively play serious roles in an infant's life. It also reveals that the kid is loved even beyond their own immediate family. This can allow them to learn 3 particular basic values, loyalty, responsibility, and independence.

This is important not only for children and young people themselves, but also for their families, friends, and the societies they reside and form relationships in.

As my mom always says, kids are like flowers, they bloom when nurtured properly but a touch of force will bruise them forever. I love this saying,

"The way we talk to our children becomes their inner voice."

Peggy O'Mara

4: Your Extended Family

For me, there is no difference between my immediate or extended family. I am blessed with so many loving relations and all of them are very close to me. As I spoke about my uncle George, I am close with all my aunts, uncles, grandparents, cousins, and their spouses. When I moved away from them is when I comprehended the loss I had endured. But I know this is not usually the case with everyone.

There are many benefits to sustaining an extended family system. Families with extended relations most definitely affect the outcome of a child's behavior and character and have access to a more thorough upbringing. These families relay the beliefs and policies of modern society in a very concentrated way. Therefore, this lets the kids have much more experience and exposure to different interests and ideas that are significant life lessons that parents may not have the time, patience, or ability to teach like cultural identity and a sense of community. The diverse skills, abilities, and knowledge of a large family can be of great help. No single person can know it all or acquire virtually all the aptitudes and abilities of an institution as a whole. Assistance is usually ready from the family when expected in an emergency or even in projects and activities. Weddings, birthdays, bar mitzvahs, and funerals, are all expected to be attended by the whole family members and this is when one acknowledges the importance of family, immediate or extended.

But it is a given that, to every advantage, there would be disadvantages. Disagreements and conflicts are almost unavoidable within extended families. Most disputes may arise when there is a lack of mutual understanding among members. There are times when too much care for someone can lead to conflict and jealousy. Grandparents may violate their boundaries and make parents feel inefficient. But it's not so bad, there are so many ways to revive truce between them. The remedy is pretty easy once everyone is willing to be cooperative and appreciate that everyone has different opinions in achieving particular tasks. This admission will prevent any issues that may arise. It all comes back to mutual respect for one another. Nowadays, families are spread far and wide over the globe and physical closeness is rare but modern-day technologies make it possible for people to interact with their loved ones anytime they desire. You should take advantage of this technological advancement and keep in touch with everyone you were attached to and make sure to establish communication. Although I agree that sustaining an extended family relationship isn't that simple, whether it is from a long distance or from nearby, it takes work on the part of all the parties included, just like any other good relationship. It's a two-way street and you need to put a certain amount of effort into it. Just keep in mind that it doesn't matter that you don't get your way or everyone has to agree with your beliefs, what matters is the quality of time spent with your extended family.

There's an old saying: "It takes a village to raise a child." It may not be so today but it certainly helps and the exposure our other relations give us can never be overlooked.

5: Your Friends

"No man is an island." This observation which is credited to the famous writer John Donne has to be true. Everyone craves friendship at a point in their lives. Sometimes you desperately need a few words of encouragement or comfort from someone close to you to make the world right again, and who better than a dear friend to deliver those comments?

Did you know that a recent Harvard study learned that having solid friendships in our life even helps improve brain health?

The people we include in our lives as friends can teach us how to forgive, laugh, and make conversation. The basic part of any relationship, from our spouses to our coworkers, from cousins to neighbours, is originated from friendship. We discover how to associate with people because of our friends, even the ones that are different from us or share an unusual perspective.

Having a good number of friends lets us realize that some friendships will not last forever but each one bears something special. We learn more about ourselves and teach us how important it is to have someone, just one individual, who knows and understands you. This is the solution to getting rid of loneliness. But friends do not alleviate loneliness, they can be companions who help us during our lonely periods. By spending time with friends, we pack our lives with wonderful exchanges, heartfelt compassion, support, and laughter. When we plunge into hard times, friends are there to put things in perspective and help us out. When we succeed, they're gleaming at our promising future. Friends make us see the good in people and open us up to the possibility of sincerity in others without a personal interest. Our friends have no expectations from us and they do not need anything in return except respect and support. Friends are those people who accept you for exactly what you are, and you can easily be yourselves in their company. If the viewpoint of your friend matches your thinking, then this friendship will surely grow stronger with every passing year.

Your friends often become the pillars of strength, and genuine friends would never do anything to stop you from attaining your full potential.

Good friends will always lead you in the right direction and will try to fix problems by eliminating negativity. No human relationship can only be etched in a pleasant, seamless, and agreeable manner. Similarly, the path of friendship has numerous ups and downs and moments of agitation and regret, but friendship is such a strong bond that it can overcome every hardship. As described by Aristotle, a perfect friendship can be achieved between good people with similar virtues. In short, friends make life worth living.

6: Your Colleagues

According to research, people who have a best friend or a good friend at work are seven times more likely to be committed to their jobs. Being naturally social, we need positive interactions and good vibes to feel better just like we need oxygen to breathe. So, it makes sense that the better our associations are at work, the happier and more productive we're going to feel. When we have good relationships with those around us our work is more enjoyable. People will agree with you more and would go along with the changes you want to implement. A better working environment allows you to focus your energy and time on new opportunities rather than keep mending broken trusts and overcoming problems. Think about it, if your boss doesn't trust you, it's unlikely that he or she will think about you when a new position opens up. Across-the-board, we all want to work with people we maintain good terms with.

We also need good working relationships with others associated with our professional circle. Customers, suppliers, and key stakeholders are all vital to our success. That is why it is important to create and retain good relations with people related to our field. The better and more effectively you communicate with those around you, the substantial your relationships will be. All good relationships depend on open, honest communication. So, whether it is sending emails and IMs, meeting face-to-face, or via a virtual network, the more we express our expectations the more we get a chance to establish a healthy working environment at our workplace. When a relationship turns bitter with someone at the office, it can wreck all other areas of your life, especially if you work in close proximity to that person. Humans are companionable by nature and when a relationship is not going as smoothly as you planned, it can leave you feeling simply demoralized, causing you to miss out on respite at home after work because you can't take your mind off the tension of the day and once you don't get the rest you earned after a hard day's work, you will less likely achieve all that you're capable of the next day or for the days to come until all is well again. Stress at work can affect you in many ways, such as inducing regular headaches, poor eating habits, exhaustion, grumpiness, and more. All of these things blend and negatively impact your life, dissuading you from being your best. But when you look at this on the flip side and see how constructive good relationships at work are, the consequences are remarkable. It is likely that at some point in your career, you will work with someone with who you get along very poorly, and this is merely going to be a part of life. The best way to deal with this is to maintain a professional and civil relationship. If you're finding it difficult to find the familiar turf and keep communication professional, then start by always keeping your word on completing deadlines. But if you are completely swamped then be upfront about it. Making a compromise is a hint to the other person that you are ready to listen to them and that their opinions matter to you. When you compromise, you can usually motivate the other person to do the same, and in this way, formulate a healthy give-and-take relationship which is good for work. A reckless statement can shatter a relationship, especially at work so avoid gossiping about someone with who you don't agree. It will hurt you in the long run. Appreciation and encouragement call goes a long way into developing good relationships so if you see good work done by your colleagues even if you are at odds with them, recognize their work and positively voice your opinion.

Whether you like it or not, your colleagues are the people you spend most of your time with. You probably see them more than you see your family and friends so be respectful and appreciative of their efforts and a time will come when you will be working among friends rather than strangers.

"Effective communication helps to keep the team working on the right projects with the right attitude."

Alex Langer

7: Strangers

As I mentioned before, I suffered from a lack of confidence and social anxiety when I was younger and it still raises its head sometimes at large social gatherings where I am supposed to mingle with countless people. I feel your pain if you are also a socially conscious person like me try to avoid big congregations. Talking to someone you don't know is uncharted territory as compared to talking to your partner, your best friend, or your mom, the unfamiliarity makes it difficult and relatively intimidating. We overthink the simple fact of striking a conversation so much so that we presume the absolute worst sometimes. We may stutter, talk too much, don't have a proper comeback for the statement, sneeze, spit, get bored, and whatnot.

Well let me tell you this, there's a difference between the anticipated result and what actually transpires. How many times have you worried about a worst-case predicament only to find out that it turned out to be much better than you believed. Just don't keep high expectations and you will be fine. People are not as negative as you might think and even if they do ignore you and try to avoid having a conversation with you then you need to think about where they are at mentally, so don't take it personally. If they passed upon the opportunity to engage with you, then they missed out on something incredible and it's their loss really, not yours. Conversing with strangers and trying to get them to feel comfortable with you may be hard and you might feel intimidated but remember that this is just like any other skill where it gets easier with practice. A few of my first conversations with strangers felt scary and awkward, but they didn't do any damage. It made me learn what I needed to work on. The best way to keep someone involved in a conversation is to express an interest in their life. Everyone likes to talk about themselves so even if you don't know much about a specific subject, keep asking questions to comprehend them. Be open, smile more, be appreciative, and make them laugh. Laughter is the best medicine and it can cure all kinds of awkwardness and uneasiness. Also, the way you treat people with who you have no relationship is what makes you the most human and reveals your moral character. It feels like giving back to society and doing something charitable in a small way. You need to accept that it will not be something you are used to, at the start. You may not fall into a familiar routine that you do with your friends or relatives but it gets easier with time and patience and in the end, you may never know, you might find your best friend or soulmate in the person you have just approached as a complete stranger.

8: Non-human buddies

Our relationships should not only be constrained to humans. Now I know that this probably cannot be the case for everyone, but we can have very positive relationships with our pets. These relationships can have a positive impact on both our physical and mental health. Our cats and dogs or whoever we want to share our living space with, are the best companions a person can have. They are loyal, loving, non-judgemental, noncritical, and just cute. Some of my best times have been spent with my pet and I encourage you, in case you suffer from loneliness or have endured a personal loss, owning a friendly pet who is always happy to see you, is the best booster of your spirits you will ever get. I don't limit this to pets, it can a personal belonging that you are attached to. A car, a house, a picture, or even a key chain, if you care for something that you have and don't misuse it, then you are mentally sustaining a relationship with it whether you find it normal or not. If you discard everything that you own or has been given to you without a care, then it shows how you may treat people around you as well.

Dos and Don'ts of Communication

1: What is Communication

Communication is a skill that we develop when we are babies. It's the very first thing taught to us by our mothers. Good communication is a critical part of all relationships and is a crucial part of any healthy partnership and coalition. Every relationship faces highs and lows, but a healthy communication method can make it easier to deal with disputes and create a stronger and healthier association. We constantly hear about the importance of communication, but we are not aware of what it is and how we can utilize good communication skills in our relationships. When you are in relationships, communication normally allows to you explain to someone else what you are enduring and what your requirements are. The act of expressing not only helps to meet your needs, but also helps you to be engaged in your relationship.

"Every act of communication is a miracle of translation."

This statement says it all.

2: The Importance of Communication

Nowadays, communication has been made easier by our modern-day technologies. Social media, calling via the internet, video call and meetings, all of these have become must in our daily lives. Being able to communicate is usually labeled as one of the most important soft skills, and there is a purpose for that. First off, if you really think about it, every system in our life is related to communication at some point, and it does not need to be verbal communication. It is the skill to listen and ask the right questions that make people prefer certain bosses or business owners while refusing other job offers, picking up the phone and calling a particular friend than the rest of them, or gravitating towards one sibling or parent instead of the other. It is the gestures or a certain vibe that fascinate a person to a stranger at a gathering, it's the eye contact that helps you appreciate how your friend feels at the moment even if they are quiet. The significance of communication skills becomes even more noticeable if you put words into your expressions or body language. Simply put, they help you connect with a person on a profound level and help you ease into a relationship, whether personal or professional, smoothly and inadvertently.

The importance of communication can be told in a very simple story. A friend of mine quit his high-paying job and now owns a pet store and he loves it but at home, he wouldn't talk a lot about it. I know that he has had a passion for animals since we were kids but his new wife didn't realize the extent of his passion and would complain to him about their resources and the timings that he kept. She basically thought that he was wasting his time on a pet store when he had the potential to do something better. Things got so intense that he sold the store just to appease his wife and ended up being miserable. He would come to the boy's night out and we could see that he was unhappy. Things started becoming uncomfortable at home as well because he didn't express his feelings to his wife. He became disinterested in everything around him and eventually separated from his wife. His lack of communication cost him his marriage and it is very unfortunate that two people who apparently love and care for each other, still lack the most basic skill that makes every relationship stronger.

Communication is such an important part of any relationship, and that includes both the verbal and nonverbal parts of your interaction. Communication is a must for each partner to get their needs met and those could be physical needs, like the need for food or emotional needs, like the need for intimate physical touch.

3: The Art of Communication

Now that we have established the importance of communication, we need to know how to do it effectively and to reap its advantages. When someone is speaking with you, notice that there's always an emotion, tone of voice, eye contact, hand gestures, a hint of a mood from them during the conversation. We have discussed the necessities of communication above but I will touch on them briefly again. You need to pay attention. I can't stress on this enough. Whenever you are having a two-way conversation, you need to listen to the other person. Not just hear them say a bunch of words but actually listen to them and figure what they mean by them. You also should share insight in a positive way. You don't have to utter the reassuring words, expressions and motions can indicate that you are on the same page. You can try to capture people's attention and contain their emotions with the act of storytelling. This potent method is invariably used not only by people with excellent communicating skills but also by big businesses and companies. I have even witnessed government institutions use this strategy which only reveals its effectiveness. Telling your side of the story in this way may help you ascertain some common ground, relate your opinion, and also engage others. The best thing about storytelling is that you can wield it in any kind of situation like at home with family, at work with colleagues, among your friends, and also in your education. You have to use your communication skills everywhere but the commendable part is how to use them in a way that helps you and others around you. I once met probably the best salesman on this planet and he works for a small brand at a mall. When I went into the store, I had no intention of buying anything. I was just waiting to meet up with a friend and wanted to kill the time. As soon as I walked in, he greeted me with a genuine smile. Then he was not on my case as most of the salespersons do. He let me roam around and when I liked something and picked it up he walked up to me and inquired politely if I wanted it in my size. I did and he brought me options to try for size, not assuming that I might be size 10 or 12. He gave me both and stepped away as I went in to try my garments. Once I was satisfied with the one I fit into I walked out and he casually handed me a matching scarf and jacket that were going excellently with the dress. As I got excited at the prospect of getting such an awesome outfit put together within minutes he cracked a few jokes and I was completely washed away by his charm. He also told me that these items were on sale and he went and got the discounted ones for me specifically. It was true, the store wasn't having a sale at the time but there was a small rack at the end which had a few items hanging from it. You wouldn't even notice it even if you passed it by. I could feel that he really wanted me to have these items before anyone else got their hands on them and ruined my perfect outfit. It was his sincerity, genuine interest, and honest opinion which were delivered in the most respectful way that blew me off my feet. As I paid for my things he offered to take my bags and put them away behind the counter until I was done with my lunch with my friend. I could get them once I was done. He walked me out and waved me goodbye. I just felt that I had had an encounter with someone really important and had gotten accepted at my ideal job. I just felt refreshed, excited, and pleased with myself and it was because of this guy who made me feel like a million dollars. There was no magic and no, he wasn't even good-looking, he was just nice! That's it.

Acting positively, using your body language to augment your opinions, and trying to engage people into relating with you by your words being sentimental yet informative is the key to good communication and is the stance of successful people all over the world.

4: Causes of Lack of Communication

Relationships are all about commitment. Commitment to move forward, to grow, to share, and to give back. But, one thing that stops all the relationships from growing and evolving is the lack of communication. It stints the development of feelings and misguided people from the path of togetherness to misunderstandings and isolation. Relationship communication problems can leave you feeling frustrated and often it seems like your loved ones don't get you. But the reasons for lack of communication are pretty insubstantial in my opinion. There is nothing that you cannot overcome if you intend to.

Being overly busy makes you sound less time with your loved ones and they may feel that you never have time for them anymore. This is such a common problem between couples and parents with their children and is the easiest to avoid. It usually takes place when one person in the relationship starts taking the other for granted. This causes a lack of communication between both the parties involved. Another issue that I have noticed is having too many expectations of each other. Our partners or friends can't always know what we feel or what we want and

116

occasionally they just can't put as much focus into the relationship as we like, for any reason, which gets in the way from time to time. If you're struggling with communication issues in a relationship then you need to dial down your expectation of others. Being overly aggressive during discussions can also stop your loved ones from voicing their feelings. If you burst out in anger or become judgemental often then you are more likely giving a signal to the other person to shit them down. Harsh words and spiteful attitude is the biggest reason for the absence of communication between two people. Keeping your feelings hidden or pent up is also a big damper on expressing yourself. It stops the other person from being honest and open because they sense unease and hesitation in you as well. The underlying emotions can erupt one day causing a lot of emotional damage to your relationships. Trying to be as clear and making things as uncomplicated as you can may help revive the lost communication between you and your loved ones. Make sure that you mend the communication between relationships before it's too late and you lose your loved ones in a frenzy of heartache and misunderstandings. You must have heard that,

"Unhealthy relationships are most commonly lacking in the most essential of ingredient: healthy communication."

Asa Don Brown

"When you stop communicating, you become poor."

Meir Ezra

5: The Effects of Communication

Good communication skills have wonderful effects on your life and as I have explained in detail, it is the basis of a healthy relationship. By maintaining normalcy in your daily life and not keeping everything bottled up inside, you build a strong and powerful connection with people you love.

Active communication cultivates trust with others. Your capacity to listen attentively and grasp different points of view boosts other people's confidence that you are making good decisions for everyone involved in your life. As you conform as a role model, this faith will extend to your loved ones and they will feel as though they can trust their families and friends more to accomplish their assigned responsibilities. Everyone must support and assist the people connected to them and we all should want the best for our closest people.

Once you establish good communication with your family and friends, it effectively plays a big part in settling disputes and dissuading possible ones from happening. The solution is to remain calm, make sure all parties are heard and find an antidote that is ideal for everyone affected by the problem. Listening carefully and proposing quality feedback enables people to feel heard and understood. This, in turn, fosters mutual respect which is a great effect of heartfelt communication. The effects can be seen not only in personal life but also in the professional one. When staff members recognize their parts, the positions of others, and your expectations and goals, they can concentrate more on their work and less on workplace issues. With open and easy communication, disagreements are concluded quickly, employees can better adjust their workload, and distractions are minimized. These privileges contribute to outstanding productivity for you and your team.

Good communication skills can play an important role in nurturing positive experiences for everyone. As people feel heard and understood by you, you naturally improve yourself and it increases your self-love and helps with your emotional well-being too. Just like I encountered the salesman and felt elated after the experience, people will feel more connected with you and will feel relaxed and comfortable in your presence. My favourite TV personality says,

"My belief is that communication is the best way to create strong relationships."

Jada Pickett Smith

6: The Effects of Miscommunication

Similar to the effects of communication, there are plenty of effects of miscommunication as well. These are some of the aftermaths of poor communication skills.

You will fall into a pit of constant fights and nagging. The fault-finding habit will cause escalated conflict and dispute in every relationship you have. You will feel that your loved ones are always wrong and the need to moan and complain about each aspect of life will eventually make you suspicious of them. You will develop a negative perspective of your relationship and would doubt their intention for you at every given chance. The habit of miscommunication will make you shy away from each other's attempts to connect and you will stop making the effort. If you are not communicating with someone you love, you endorse a feeling of being unseen or ill-conceived which can be very hurtful and damaging to your relationship. Lack of communication can also project your loved one into a lonely state. One of the worst feelings in the world is loneliness and it is the number one cause of depression and suicide in the U.S today. Scary isn't it? I know you would be thinking that just not spending time with someone and not talking to them often couldn't possibly cause such a huge mess. Well, it does. Let me tell you how.

My sister's boss is a very good lady but a great administrator. She keeps an eagle eye on everyone at the office but she doesn't leave this attitude at home and is suffering because of that. She has an iron grip on her kids and is very disciplined herself so expects everyone around her to have a strict routine too. Which, let me tell you, is not bad, it's just very authoritative of her and her family is at odds with her because of this. She has become lonely and is having trouble connecting with her family. The other day, I was shocked to learn that her husband had just packed his bags and left. He was fed with her military regime and he claimed that they rarely spent time with each other because he did not relax in her presence. It is really sad but true for people who dictate every individual in their lives. It is fantastic to have a schedule and be organized. There is no shame in wanting perfection but, to push your desires on others and expecting them to achieve unrealistic goals is unfair and takes a toll on your closest people, especially the ones that share most part of their lives with you. Lack of intimacy is another major drawback of miscommunication and homes are falling apart because of this. It enhances the incapability of setting and reaching goals and moving forward in your life and you end being miserable and hopeless. You need to think seriously about the effects lack of communication can have on your lives and start working on it right away! As they say,

"People have character strength but they lack communication skills, and that undoubtedly affects the quality of relationships as well."

Stephen R. Covey

CONCLUSION

More than 2,300 years ago, Aristotle wrote about the importance of friendships to society, and other Greek philosophers wrote about emotions and their effects on relationships. Nowadays we have many researchers who have concluded that the foundation of every relationship is good communication.

In a relationship, you're not just getting to know another person. You're getting to know yourself better. Being in a relationship can help you work out what you want and need from the people you're close with. What are you ready to compromise on? Which qualities make you flourish? What are the core values that you can't compromise on? Maybe you don't care that your partner or friend isn't into pop music the way you are, but you can't stand it when they are scared of your dog. Get to know yourself as an individual and as a partner. Knowing yourself helps you communicate better, and the other person will definitely admire that. Communication is the heart of every relationship you have had and you will ever have. It is the basis of harmony and companionship and you will be upended from normalcy and peace if you ignore this vital skill. I hope that some of my points reached home and some of you would make an extra effort to hone your communication skills to improve your relationships with all the people you love and cherish in life. I will leave you with a few of my most favourite quotes from successful people.

"when you start communicating to change people, you leave a lasting legacy. you profit from your impact, not in spite of it."

DR. MICHELLE MAZUR

"I Speak To Everyone In The Same Way, Whether He Is The Garbage Man Or The President Of The University"

ALBERT EINSTEIN